Homeschooling Essentials

A Practical Guide to Getting Started

D1508728

Dianna Broughton

Published by Carolina Homeschooler
PO Box 1421, Lancaster, SC 29721

Visit www.carolinahomeschooler.com for more information
about resources, group trips, events, and support for
homeschooling families.

Paperback edition printed July 2012 by CreateSpace
ISBN 978-1478212508
E-book edition published July 2012
Cover design by Andrew Brown

Acknowledgments

Many thanks to the homeschooling families who join me on my group trips, attend my events, hang out with me online, and answer my surveys. It has been a pleasure sharing this journey with you.

Dedication

This book is dedicated with love and gratitude to my husband and children, who roll their eyes when I mention yet another group trip I'm planning, but put up with me anyway. I love you.

Table of Contents

Introduction

This guide focuses on the practical day-to-day aspects of homeschooling. It is intended for new homeschoolers, or for those who are looking for a better way to learn with their children.

I've used a question-and-answer format to make it easier for readers to skip to the information they need. I begin with the questions newcomers ask most often—legal issues, educational requirements, record-keeping, testing, and meeting other homeschoolers. Then I discuss different types of schedules, teaching methods, favorite resources, and how to manage the high school years. I finish with advice for handling problems you may encounter along the way, and include a few good articles for inspiration.

I'm grateful to the homeschoolers who answered my surveys, shared their wisdom and experiences, and freely gave advice to help me make this a more useful resource. Although responses may have been lightly edited for length or clarity, their opinions are their own. I think you'll enjoy reading them as much as I have.

Please email me at director@carolinahomeschooler.com if you have a question I didn't answer, find a typo or broken link, or have comments and suggestions for future updates.

For more information about our online community, events, and group trips, visit our website at carolinahomeschooler.com. We'd love for you to join us!

Part I—Getting Started

I've decided to homeschool my children. How do I start?

Begin by researching the homeschool law for your state. It's usually best not to call your local school for legal information. Homeschooling is usually under the state's purview, so your local district may not have an accurate or complete understanding of the law.

Instead, contact a homeschool support group in your area (a list is available at home-school.com/groups). Most state groups have legal information on their websites, along with a practical "translation" of the law. There may be different interpretations, however, so try to research several sites for a more complete and balanced view of the legalities in your area.

Depending on what your state requires, you may need to register through your Department of Education or with a homeschool organization before you begin homeschooling. Some require you to complete an application that describes the methods and resources you'll be using, send a copy of your children's immunization records, or jump through other hoops. Others require only a notice of your intention to homeschool. Most fall somewhere in between the two extremes. Make sure you thoroughly understand your state's requirements so you don't run into legal issues after you withdraw your children from school.

Can I start homeschooling after the school year begins? How do I withdraw my children from school?

In most states, if not all, you can begin homeschooling at any point during the year. Your support group's website should include information about the withdrawal process, or you can call your school district to ask for their preferred procedure. (To avoid inadvertently violating attendance laws, I recommend obtaining legal homeschool status before you withdraw your children from school.)

If there is no established withdrawal procedure for your school, I recommend sending a certified letter to your district's superintendent and the principal of the school your children currently attend. Explain you are withdrawing your children (state your children's names, and the date of withdrawal) from their school and are educating them at home according to your state's homeschool regulations. Sign the letter and keep a copy (with proof of certified mailing) in case you are asked to provide documentation later. If your children attend a private school, it should be enough to simply inform them you're withdrawing your children to begin homeschooling.

If you decide to wait until after the school year ends to homeschool, there's usually no need to officially withdraw your children. Just make sure you're legally registered to homeschool in your state (start the process at the beginning of summer vacation in case of delays), and don't re-enroll them in public or private school when the new school year begins.

What subjects do I need to teach? What are the requirements for each grade level?

Some states require specific subjects for each grade, while others leave it up to the parent. If your state allows you to choose your own subjects, focus on the broad areas of reading/literature, writing, history/social studies, science, and mathematics. The arts (music, drawing, theater, etc.) often aren't mandated, but are worthwhile areas of study nonetheless. Each of the broader areas can be narrowed down even further: American literature, composition, health/physical education, world history, choir, grammar, state history, geography, biology, algebra, etc.

Many "experts" disagree about what children should learn and when. Some advocate early academics, while others believe imaginative play during the early years is more important and encourage a "better late than early" approach to academics.

I was a typical "military brat," traveling from place to place throughout my school years. I went to four or five different elementary schools, and three different middle schools. Each varied widely in its emphasis on academics, art, music, sports, and other areas. With every move, I was considered behind in some areas, and advanced in others, yet I still managed to graduate at the normal age, go to college, and eventually get a master's degree. So don't stress too much if your child hasn't memorized the multiplication facts by a certain grade. He'll know them by the time he graduates.

If you want an idea of what is usually taught at different grade levels, I recommend World Book's Typical Course of Study (worldbook.com/typical-course-of-study). Keep in mind it's just a summary of what's generally taught in the schools that answer their survey, so use it only as a guide.

What records do I need to keep?

Many states require you to document what your children are learning during the year. When you register to homeschool, you should receive information about the records you'll need to keep. Your state or local support group's website will also likely have examples and forms posted on their website. If not, here are some typical formats:

Journals and Plan Books

A journal (or diary) is used to document topics and activities after your children complete them. This method is great for families who have a relaxed, child-led, or unschooling approach. You don't know what each day will bring, so recording the details at the end of the day (or week) makes sense. It's easy and parent-friendly, but can also cause stress if you need a plan to stay focused and feel like you're accomplishing something.

A plan book (or calendar) is used to list each day's activities in advance. This approach is good for those who feel more comfortable having a "plan of attack." The downside is you may feel overwhelmed and behind if you don't complete the entire list every day. It also inhibits "free-range" learning (allowing your children to explore topics of interest in depth) because you're focused on checking off the tasks on your list.

If neither method seems quite right for you, start with a combination of the two and adjust from there. Just write a bare skeleton (perhaps weekly goals), and allow yourself and your children to be flexible within those goals. Fill in the details as they accomplish each task and add new ideas and opportunities as they arise.

Portfolios

A portfolio is simply a folder containing samples of your student's work. If you use a structured curriculum, include a few worksheets, assignments, and tests each semester from all subject areas. These samples should portray your student's best work and show a progression of skills and topics learned throughout the year.

If you don't use worksheets or tests, you'll need to get more creative. For reading/literature, you may want to include a reading list with a brief summary or review of each book. For writing, include samples of your student's written work: stories, essays, poems, riddles, copies of letters they've written to family or friends, reports, research papers, etc.

For social studies, consider including a list of books (historical fiction and nonfiction), movies, magazines, documentaries, as well as brochures and pictures from field trips. Also include a sample of written work—a journal your student kept during a trip to Colonial Williamsburg, for example, or a report describing the history of a local monument or statue.

Use the same approach with science (brochures and pictures from field trips, photos of experiments or projects, notes and results of experiments, a list of books, magazines, and documentaries, etc.).

Progress Reports

Progress reports may be required at specific intervals during the year (every six weeks, at the end of each semester, or whatever your state mandates). Reporting methods can consist of a simple report card, or a more detailed summary of topics studied during the preceding assessment period.

The summary approach emphasizes your student's educational activities and topics studied, while report cards focus more on grades. If you prefer to use report cards, you can use the terms "excels," "satisfactory," and "needs improvement" for younger students, and letter grades for middle school students.

Assessing progress at the high school level becomes more involved if your student is planning to go to college. A grade point average, which requires a numerical grading scale, is usually required for scholarship applications. See the high school section in this book for more information about determining grades, transcripts, and other topics.

Donna Young's website is a good place to get forms for report cards, progress reports, journals, planners, and more. To download these forms, visit donnayoung.org/index.htm.

Are we required to test at the end of the year?

It depends on your state. Some states require testing every year, while others require it less often, or not at all. If you have a choice, keep in mind that testing has very little to do with learning.

Most standardized tests are intended for public school students, not homeschoolers, so they don't accurately reflect the broad range of knowledge that is typical of our students. Since we don't "teach to the test," our children often study subjects that aren't included on most standardized tests.

To further decrease their usefulness, most of the tests have time limits. This penalizes our students, who aren't as experienced working under conditions with artificial time restrictions. We prefer to let them think through problems, valuing quality and accuracy over speed. (After all, there are few situations where doing a complex math problem in five seconds flat will ever be a life or death situation.)

To complicate matters even more, the science and social studies sections usually cover very specific topics each year. Your children may not score well in those areas if they didn't study the same subject. (The fifth-grade test may cover American history, for example, but your 5th-grader studied ancient history.)

So what's the use in testing? The scores will give you a general idea of how your child is doing in certain subjects when compared to public school students. Also, good test scores tend to reassure family and friends, who may not be as comfortable with homeschooling as you are.

If you choose to test, or are required to, try to reduce stress by skipping the science and social studies sections (if your state allows it), or choose a test that doesn't assess those subjects. Focus instead on reading, language arts, and math. These areas are more skill-related, and depend less on content that may change from year to year.

If you can't skip sections, research what topics are covered on the test and review them with your children beforehand. Also, let your children take a practice test first so they can become more comfortable with the format and time limitations. (See the list of companies below for test preparation materials.)

After you get the results, keep in mind what they really mean. If your elementary-age children scored at a high school level in math, it doesn't mean that they're ready for algebra. It just means they answered as many questions correctly as the high school students who were used to norm the test. They may not actually have the abstract reasoning skills needed for algebra yet. You'll know when your children are ready to progress to each stage of learning. Don't let the test scores replace your own judgment.

I've listed several test providers below. Before you decide on a test, check your state law to see if specific tests are required and whether you need a certified teacher or administrator to give the test. (Many tests can be given by the parent, at home.)

Seton Testing Services
www.setontesting.com

Bayside School Services
www.baysideschoolservices.com

Bob Jones University
www.bjupress.com/testing

Family Learning Organization
www.familylearning.org/testing.html

What about socialization?

This is the question I'm asked most often, which is ironic because socialization is discouraged in public schools. How many times did you hear "We're not here to socialize!" when *you* were a kid? Nothing has changed—students are still hearing the same thing today. And in my area, they've eliminated or shortened recess periods, assemblies, and other social activities during school hours in favor of more time for academics.

If you're concerned your children will have problems because they're not out in the "real world," ask yourself if being in a room with 25 same-aged peers for 180 days a year is truly a real-world situation. As homeschoolers, your children will interact with people of all ages and backgrounds, in a variety of settings, throughout the year. Which is more "real?" Which group is really more "socialized?"

According to researchers, the homeschoolers are. Studies have found that our students are typically more mature than their public-school peers, exhibiting fewer behavioral problems and a greater ability to interact positively with a wider variety of ages, including adults. (These findings are documented in the thesis titled "The Socialization of Homeschool Children" by Thomas Smedley, M.S. and the dissertation titled "Comparison of Social Adjustment Between Home and Traditionally Schooled Students" by Dr. Larry Shyers, in addition to other studies not cited in this guide.)

Your children can participate in organized activities such as 4-H, local recreation leagues, scouts, church events, etc. For interaction with other homeschoolers, parents around the country have gone a step further to coordinate their own learning co-operatives, field trips, sports teams, and more (see carolinahomeschooler.com/atravel.html for a list of group trips available to homeschoolers around the country). The reality is your children may have more opportunities to socialize in the "real world" than they can comfortably fit into their schedules.

We're enrolled in a virtual charter school through our state. Are we homeschoolers?

No. Your children are public school students who access their state curriculum from home. You can't choose your own materials and your children must adhere to your state's requirements and daily/hourly attendance rules. They must answer to a certified teacher who monitors their progress, and must participate in statewide testing.

Homeschoolers aren't public school students, and don't have to answer to an outside teacher. We have much more freedom to choose curriculum, subjects, methods of assessment, and can set our own attendance schedule.

I'm not saying (or implying) that homeschooling is better (or worse) than virtual charter schooling. It's a legal distinction that must remain clear to protect our rights as homeschoolers. I believe that the focus should be on what's best for our children, not on which method is "better."

Part II—Schedules & Typical Days

Do I have to follow a regular school schedule?

One of the biggest advantages of homeschooling is the freedom to integrate learning into our daily lives. Some states require parents to teach a specific number of days each year (usually around 180) and a minimum number of hours per day, but you get to decide which days and which hours.

You can follow a traditional school calendar if you want (August to May, Monday through Friday, 8:00 am to 3:00 pm, complete with recess and lunch breaks). Or you can homeschool year-around, schedule three weeks on and one week off, or four days a week. You can include weekends, work around a second- or third-shift schedule, or do whatever fits your family's lifestyle. Homeschooling can be as flexible as you need it to be.

When you're counting days (and hours, if required by your state), remember that learning happens all the time. If you visit your local zoo, museum, aquarium, or historical park this weekend, count it as a field trip. If you go to educational attractions while you're on vacation, add them to your list. If your children have conversations with relatives and friends about their experiences in the Vietnam War or growing up during the Great Depression, you can document that, too.

Also, what takes an hour to learn in a school setting takes less time at home because you don't have a student/teacher ratio of 25-to-1. You won't have the interruptions, the behavior problems, or the crowd control issues that public school teachers do. And, incidentally, your children will never again have to raise their hand and ask for permission to go to the restroom. That alone is worth the price of admission. Just sayin'.

What does a typical homeschool day look like?

Schedules vary depending on whether a family uses a "school-at-home" textbook approach or a completely relaxed, child-led, or "unschooling" approach (these methods, and others, are described in the next section).

To give you an idea of how much variation there is, I asked homeschooling moms and dads to describe their typical days. Although I couldn't include all of their replies, these represent the diversity of the families who participate in my online community. Some have strict daily schedules, while others have no schedule at all. I hope reading about them will help you develop a schedule that best suits your family.

Unstructured Days

We don't really have a typical homeschooling day. Every day is different. This morning we are watching reruns of Beakman's World on Netflix while I recover from a couple of days spent at the hospital with my mom. We love field trips and try to go somewhere every week. I believe the best learning takes place outside the classroom, so we try to take advantage of trips and other opportunities to see and do new things. When we are at home, my children (eight and ten) might do two to three hours of book-type work, then we throw in some free reading, lots of outside play, building with Legos, science or building projects, or whatever strikes our fancy! —Amy, Georgia

We don't have a "typical" homeschooling day. I strive to do a few hours a week. I believe that my children are learning all the time, even when we are not sitting in the schoolroom doing specific activities. We find learning moments in almost every activity—even grocery shopping! I also have a very active three-year-old, and a lot of our schooling (particularly learning new subjects) is done when she is napping or otherwise occupied. If it is a subject or discussion that I believe all three will enjoy, then I build age-appropriate activities for all three of them. —Rebecca, Michigan

We wake up when rested, then pursue whatever is calling us at the time: yardwork, inventions, internet play or research, cooking, music, travel, cycling, animals, meditation, reading, writing, games, artwork, building or design, correspondence, sports or physical activity, gardening, cloud- and star-gazing. Busy days! —Kelly, South Carolina

It varies from day to day, but my child and I are not morning people, so we tend to start off curled up in bed or on the porch reading, doing math, or watching educational videos. Of course, this changes when we leave earlier for field trips or classes. If we stay focused, we can get a lot of work done in our subject area, but sometimes we just get distracted by whatever happens to catch our attention. In the late afternoons and evenings, my daughter has practices and rehearsals with her musical theater troupe. She takes tap/jazz, ballet, and voice in addition to the troupe class. —Deb, South Carolina

I set them to a task and let them run around the house and play every time they finish something. Then we go back to the table, or kitchen, or scouts, or homeschool co-op, or guitar lessons. We take week-long trips to Williamsburg, Washington DC, Gran Gran's house, the beach, and the mountains, and we see every "student rate" play offered at the local arts center and theater—eight plays a year. We are astonished when they ask who's there for the first time and so many hands go up. We take frequent field trips to museums, festivals, etc., usually in costumes for extra fun. In the afternoon, they play and then must finish up any leftover work after play time. We have an hour now and then for intense house cleaning, and we hold a laundry party, where we fold and hang the clean clothes. My 12-year-old has full understanding of washing duds. Our schedule is loose, and that flexibility can be scary, but I trust that eventually they will be ready for life and love. —Kerry, Georgia

All our days are different, but most include some time reading, some time with visual media, and time in the world away from home. We listen to audiobooks and stories (especially Jim Weiss) in the car. —Heather, Virginia

We travel a great deal, so our schedule depends on several factors. We discuss our plans at the beginning of each day. We typically have a project in the works, currently a small book we're writing about places we have been. Today, we decided to start with math, then continue with the book. My son likes to keep going on something once he starts it, so if we get on a roll, math may take several hours. During this time, I am usually doing my own work and just stay nearby to help if needed. We take breaks to eat, get outside for a little while, or watch TV. The book project is all encompassing—writing, reading, drawing illustrations, and may take several hours. It could be science all day, or an audio book and worksheets, or a day spent outdoors. We're always flexible. —Christina, Ohio

Our schedule really varies. Some days are pretty structured and other days are just wide open. Last week, nobody was motivated to do much, so we watched some Nova videos and called it a day. But then other days, we'll spend the entire day tightly focused on a particular subject. And then there will be other days where my son will decide to spend the entire day working on a book he's been writing (he's up to 11 chapters now). —Jamy, North Carolina

Our days are pretty different, but here are some examples of what my daughter will do in a typical day: visit some community place (museum, art studio, play, concert, nature center, etc.), spend time with a homeschooled friend, work on her eBay business (listing, emailing, packing, shipping, etc.), play Sims and Minecraft, watch YouTube videos for leisure or education, prepare meals, practice violin (usually several times a day), practice dance, choreograph dances, do art projects or science experiments, then attend that evening's activity (depending on the night—gymnastics team practice, dance class, violin lesson, orchestra). —Pam, Illinois

Semi-Structured Days

We try to do our "textbook" work, such as math, first. Then if we decide to watch a program on baby sloths for science, or a documentary about WWII, we can sit back with some popcorn and enjoy that learning time a little more relaxed. Some days I ask my son what he wants to start with and let him dictate the order of things. There have been times when he's so into a book, he just wants to read (and read, and read) in the morning. I usually just go with that, even if other subjects don't get their time in that day. He has been involved in band, fencing, horseback riding, archery, art classes, and Junior Achievement BizTown. We focus on core curriculum before lunch and electives after lunch. Our annual highlight is "Practical Math & Science" between Thanksgiving and Christmas. No textbooks, just lots of fun, but the learning never stops—from learning how to organize recipes into grocery lists (writing), to shopping (math), to measuring (math), to baking (science), to delivery (the ultimate life-lesson: giving!). —Tara, Tennessee

We travel a lot, so there is no typical homeschool day in our life. The days we are home, we start around nine and are done usually around one. We do Bible, language arts, math, and history every day when we're at home. We alternate nature study, picture study, art, Shakespeare, and poetry once or twice a week. —Carmen, North Carolina

The kids are up at 8:00 am to feed the chickens and horses, and to ride their horses. Then they come back inside for breakfast, which they usually make themselves. They are also responsible for cleaning up the kitchen. After that, it's music practice for 30 minutes (cello, violin, piano) and Teaching Textbooks for 30 minutes. Sometimes they'll ask for help with a math concept, but usually they can grasp it on their own. By this time it's usually noon or so, and they are free to do whatever they'd like, usually they read. We have tons of books in the house—textbooks, fiction, historical. Currently they are into anything involving werewolves or vampires. I also try to find at least 30 minutes to read aloud to them a book of my choice. Computer time is limited to an hour or two per day, but they do like to play Minecraft. (If they are writing stories using the word processor, I don't limit their time.) They do swim team and soccer, depending on the season. We also take lots of trips! —Ann, South Carolina

The older kids do a little work with me on basic subjects like math and English, but they do a lot of independent work, too. The youngest spends, at most, an hour working with me on math and English, the rest of her time is spent letting her ask questions and learn by playing. We read a lot together; myths are big right now. —Betsy, North Carolina

The kids have lists of what they can do on their own for the week. They start on those lists right after breakfast. Then I call them individually to read to them or help with any work that is more difficult. We are very flexible though. If it's a gorgeous day, I might let them play outside all morning and then we'll work on school in the afternoon. School fits into our life; we don't work our life around school. —Alison, South Carolina

There is no typical day! My kids are in a variety of homeschool classes and activities, so each day varies. If we're home all day, we start around 11:00 am (we are not morning people) and do around three hours of schoolwork. Then my daughter practices piano. When her father comes home, she does an hour or so of math with him. —Stephanie, Georgia

Structured Schedules

We get up around 8:00 am, settle into work by 9:00 am, and try to finish up "book work" by noon. Then we move on to projects and passions. We take lots of day trips and other outside educational experiences. We do some co-op classes, mostly for enrichment, like science labs or literature discussion. —Leigh, Alabama

A typical day involves math, English, Latin, and spelling. We have brief breaks in between, as needed, where we go outside and find lizards, ride scooters, or play baseball. In the afternoons, we usually have sports, swim, outdoor time, science time, socialize, and play piano. —Kate, South Carolina

Is there such a thing as a typical homeschooling day? Just about every day is different for us because of activities, such as homeschool group, swim and gym class, band, violin and trumpet lessons, orchestra, field trips, etc. On most days, we get up by 8:00 am and begin school around 9:00 am. We switch between book work, computer work and hands-on work as the curriculum dictates or my boys need to hold their attention. Depending on the day, we may need to run to an activity after a couple hours of book work, but then we return in the afternoon to finish anything left undone. —Cathy, Indiana

We usually start at 8:30 am. We begin our day with Bible and another class, and then my son takes a 15-minute break. He goes outside or stretches his legs somehow. We do a couple more classes and then take a one-hour lunch break. After that, we finish our day usually around 2:30 pm. We head out to the YMCA or library after school a few times a week. —Jennifer, South Carolina

From 8:45 am to 12:30 pm we do a combination of writing, math, science, and any projects the children are working on. In the afternoon, we have swimming, hockey, computer programming, art, field trips, making a fort in the backyard, and biking—basically things the children enjoy doing and don't realize they are doing "school" —Diana, Ontario, Canada

We have morning chores, then Bible study, then hit the books. I am lucky now that my kids are older. I tell them what needs to be completed and they come to me when they have questions. We love field trip days. I am always looking for the latest and greatest field trips. We also have two awesome co-ops in our area where my kids learn Spanish, sign language, and all sorts of other classes that I might not have the skills to teach. —Monica, South Carolina

We have a devotional time following breakfast. Then my 14-year-old will usually get started on her day's lessons, completing most of them on her own. I work with my 9-year-old son to complete his daily assignments. We use Beautiful Feet for our history, so we do the majority of the reading for that as a group. I usually read aloud while they listen and complete the study guide questions. We are typically finished by lunchtime or early afternoon. —Sarah, North Carolina

Each day starts with math since that's our most difficult subject. If it goes well, it's behind us early in the day, and if it doesn't, we can take a break and come back to it later. After that, I generally let my son decide the order, depending on what we are doing. He loves civics and science, so they usually follow math. Literature is a family activity, so we do it together in the evenings. We've been renovating the house the past few weeks, so he has been earning shop credits for sanding, painting, etc. Monday is community service day. My son has helped deliver Meals-on-Wheels for ten years now. We usually get out of the house on Thursdays, which means anything from a hike in the woods, to a tour of the Carl Sandburg home, or a visit to Biltmore House. —Kim, South Carolina

We usually start around 9:00 am. On Monday through Thursday, we do reading, spelling, phonics, and handwriting. We take a short break for a snack, then do math and any other supplementals we have for the day. Fridays are reserved for science and social studies. —Courtney, North Carolina

We start with textbook work (four subjects), then do physical education. We finish up the other subjects after lunch. My students work one day a week in an internship. Usually we have school only half the day on Friday, which is our day to get together with other friends to do field trips. We also have one day a week when we help others with a task. But the best part about homeschooling is the wonderful flexibility to change our days and go on adventures to learn. When my children reach the age of 16 we give them the option to take college courses for dual enrollment. Both of my older children have done this and have done very well. My oldest graduated with a Bachelor of Science at age 20. —Sharon, Virginia

We start each morning at 9:00 am. We try to get math done first, then writing, because they are my son's least favorite subjects. Then we continue with history, reading, spelling, science, musical instruments, and exercising. We do every subject every day. My son is given a checklist of what needs to be completed for the week. If he completes them early, we take Friday off for something fun. —Stephanie, South Carolina

My child needs alone time first thing in the morning, so I give him time to wake up and get motivated for our day. After our morning chores and breakfast, we start "school" around 10:00 am. I plan ahead what we will work through that day and week, and we just jump in. I know ahead of time what field trip or outside enrichment classes are coming up, and we plan accordingly. We work through our core classes and anything else I have planned for that day until they are completed. Some days are faster than others, and that's okay. —Kimberly, South Carolina

My 16-year-old is now working on her own, handling her schedule and schoolwork herself. With my 9-year-old, we have Bible reading first, then we read-aloud from three living books (covering science, American history, and world history), with a math and spelling lesson in between readings. Then we work on art, penmanship, or writing. We're usually finished around lunch time. After lunch he has free time to read on his own, play outside, build with Legos (or scrap wood, outside), etc. We have no video games and we watch very, very little TV, so he is forced to use his imagination and creativity. —Nancy, North Carolina

We're very relaxed and have a rhythm rather than a schedule. We wake up, have breakfast, make beds, then start our morning work. We do math and language arts first, then free reading. We have a snack around 10:30 am, and finish up with science, history, or art. We finish around lunch time. —Bethany, Tennessee

My oldest is in high school, so most of her work is done alone. She will often sit in the den with the other two while everyone does their own work. My other two are upper elementary and they start off the day doing their math and language arts. Then they listen to their history on CD. We usually do science, Bible, and poem memorization together, and then in the afternoon they read. We do art, music, and field trips on Fridays.—Melissa, South Carolina

Student-Directed Schedules

There really isn't a typical day. A lot depends on what is going on outside of home. The boys (12 and 10) usually decide what they are going to accomplish first (giving them that decision makes everything much easier). My daughter works independently these days. Basically, we work, read, try to get some chores done, get meals prepared, then get the children to various activities. —Zoe, South Carolina

I have a list of all of our subjects and my daughter chooses the order she wants to do them, with the exception of math. I require her to do at least half of her math before lunch. I've found she does so much better on math problems if we don't wait too late in the day to do it. We have daily exercise in the afternoons and drama once a week. Friday is a shorter day due to spending time with our homeschool group. —Donna, Georgia

What typical day? I let them get up on their own (unless they have volunteering or a field trip) and I let them decide which subjects to do when. I typically have to prod one or both to do math. —Tricia, Indiana

I let our son choose the order of his school day instead of making him follow a schedule. We usually do each class for an hour, then whatever he doesn't complete during school time is completed after school. This is due to some ADD and daydreaming characteristics of our son. We have breaks during the day to go outside and get some exercise. —Kelly, South Carolina

Teen-Oriented Schedules

Our schedule changes depending on the time of year, etc. We start later now because my daughter is a teen and likes to sleep in. We try to get bookwork done in the morning and early afternoon, leaving late afternoons for get-togethers, group classes, or field trips. We start a bit earlier in the year than public school and finish earlier by about two weeks, taking breaks at different times during the year.—Aubyn, Ontario, Canada

We started out on a schedule, starting school by 9:00 am and finishing by lunchtime or shortly after. As my boys turned into teens and became more nocturnal, our schedule relaxed and their ability to get their school done independently increased. So I dropped the timed schedule, give them their assignments, and allow them to complete them on their own time. Reminders are needed throughout the day, but they complete their assignments. We also spend many days doing school in the car when things happen that require us to drive great distances. We have always participated in a homeschool group that meets one day a week, so that keeps the boys on track and makes them accountable to someone other than their mother. —Susan, Michigan

Our typical day now that we have high schoolers is very different. My daughter is an independent student now, so on Mondays she sets up her own schedule for the week. She is very good at assessing the amount of time she needs for each subject. She starts around 9:00 am with math. She focuses on grammar, writing, and history on Monday and Tuesday; Latin, chemistry, and research on Wednesday and Thursday, and Friday is usually devoted to testing and labs. —Jackie, Georgia

Kid-Juggling Schedules

We start around 9:00 am after morning routines are complete. I work with the 6-year-old while the older two are finishing chores. We do calendar, math, phonics, and Awana. Then we do history together, including mapping, timeline work, narration, and read-alouds. Then the older two work on English, art, music, foreign language, math, and science. They usually finish between 1:00 and 2:00 pm. I finish up with science, including narration, notebooking, lapbooking, and experiments with the youngest. We spend the afternoons playing outside and most evenings are spent in organized extracurricular activities (dance, recreation center ball, and swim team.) We all read independently before bed. —Denise, North Carolina

We begin our day with our daily Bible reading and lesson, and then we cover any of our "together" subjects. After that, I have my older child work on any independent work while I work with my youngest. When my youngest has accomplished her work for the day, we will do a simple craft (my oldest can join in if she wants). Then I work with my oldest in any areas she might need help with. —Kellie, Kentucky

I'm not sure we ever have a typical homeschooling day. Because my 4-year-old has special needs and we have help who comes each morning for two hours to work with her, I try to use that time to work on any assignments my 3rd-grader can't do independently. I choose the order of these assignments so I can make sure we get to the most important assignments each day. (We run short on time because I tend to overplan.) During this time my 8th-grader completes assignments independently in whatever order she chooses. After our help leaves, I try to set up the 4-year-old with some fun stuff to do (nothing formal or too structured this year) while I go over any assignments my 8th-grader needs help with, and my 3rd-grader completes independent work in whatever order she chooses, and assists the 4-year-old, if necessary. We try to save extracurricular activities for afternoons so mornings are committed to studies. —Rose, South Carolina

There's no typical day around here. I try to get up and exercise before the younger kids wake up. The youngest are up and fed by 9:00 am, I drag the oldest out of bed between 9:00 and 10:00 am, harass them to do their morning chores, and get them on task for the day. The oldest three have outlines that list what they need to complete for the week. We try to do read-alouds and group subjects before lunch, then round up the middle two for seat work. The oldest (finishing 8th grade) does most of her work in her room, much of it late at night. I try to keep the 3-year-old occupied and out of trouble while working with the other three. She has some "special" toys but sometimes we resort to NickJr.com or a DVD on the laptop in the next room. I try to finish with the middle two by mid-afternoon so we can get to ball practice, gymnastics, park day, and get dinner together before daddy gets home. —Ellen, Georgia

My middle child self-directs her day very well, so I work with her as needed, while guiding my youngest with math, phonics, etc. My oldest usually gets up later than rest, then works on his own in his room. We sometimes have outside activities, such as scouts, in the evening. Twice a week we have music lessons or gym classes at the YMCA. We try to travel with my husband several times a year, and go to a lot of museums and interesting places. —Candace, South Carolina

Each child, beginning with the youngest, gets 30-40 minutes of one-on-one time with me. We work on anything they can't do on their own. The other kids work on their individual subjects and do their free-reading while I work with one child. We break for lunch from 12-1:30 pm. From 1:30-3:00 pm, we work together as a group on science or Story of the World, in a rotating Monday/Wednesday and Tuesday/Thursday schedule. —Shannon, Maryland

I work with my middle child while the older one works on his own thing (not strictly school-related) or plays with his younger brother. When we are done, the middle child plays with the younger one, and the older one does his work. Usually my oldest can work independently, but for those times when we work together, we plan for a time when the other two are playing nicely. The youngest isn't really "school-age," but he absorbs quite a bit as he plays and listens to the lessons for the older ones. When we have days when no one can focus and everything seems to be going wrong, we take a day off and use it to work in the garden or do something fun together, and that's okay, too. —Michelle, Pennsylvania

Work-Juggling Schedules

My wife and I have a home cleaning business, so our son goes with us. He does his school work at each house, getting most of it finished by the time we are done. We leave the house at 7:30 am most mornings. If we're scheduled to work later, school starts at 7:15 am when we have the pledge and a character trait with a Bible verse, then prayer. I spend the afternoon checking work and assisting my son where needed. —John, South Carolina

I work at home, so I get up around 8:00 am and do about an hour of work. The kids get up around 9:00 am and we usually start slow, with reading or something easy. Then we just go through our schedule that I've (hopefully) organized beforehand, and finish around 2:00 pm or so. Once a week or two, we try to do a nature walk and art. I like My Father's World curriculum because it includes music, art projects, and nature walks. We have a relaxed homeschool. The challenge is not to stress out about being relaxed! —Julie, Georgia

What's typical? There are days when I have to work, so we just get our history, science, literature readings, and math done. Some days I stay home all day and we get more accomplished. Sometimes my daughter does more work than usual on her own. We live our lives, and fit school into it, not the other way around. It's one of the things I had to learn to embrace, because if we didn't complete everything on the "list" every day, I was so uptight! —Lara, South Carolina

Since I work full-time and my husband works evenings (but doesn't like to teach), my son does work I leave for him, with my husband supervising most days. On other days, my son participates in area enrichment classes. —Susan, North Carolina

My husband and I both work full-time, so we split the subjects. He does the core math, English, spelling, and handwriting lessons during the weekdays and I do science, history, and reading in the evenings. We take homeschool classes at our local science center, zoo, public parks, gym class, and the art museum. We don't have a schedule each day. Sometimes we do stuff on the weekends as well. We go all year and take breaks for holidays and vacations. —Pamela, Ohio

Each day I start out by correcting the previous day's work and printing assignments for the day. I don't accept scores lower than 80%, so if there's something they need to correct, I reassign that. If they need to watch DVDs or do experiments, I make sure everything is available. While one of the kids is working on the computer, the other is doing their math or non-computer-related work. Chores are done throughout the day. I leave at 1:00 pm to go to work and don't get back until 10:00 pm. During that time, they finish up assignments or do their chores. When I come home, we go over anything they had trouble with. On my days off, I purchase or assemble any supplies needed for the following week and review any subjects the kids aren't grasping. We school all year, but take time off whenever we feel the need. Dad is a long-haul trucker, so he isn't home a lot. When he comes home, we do family things. One of the perks of homeschooling is being able to adjust your schedule as needed. —Debi, Utah

We don't differentiate weekends in our house. My husband has an irregular schedule and often works weekends, so any day is a potential homeschool day or recreation day. We travel a lot. We probably take a trip out of state each month. That is one of the benefits of homeschooling that we love—the freedom to travel. —Lisa, North Carolina

Appointment-Juggling Schedules

Our schedule mostly depends on who has an appointment, and what type of appointment it is. If we are at home, we do math, language arts, grammar, social studies or science, writing, and reading. If we are going out for an appointment, we may do only a little of their workbooks, then read in the car. It varies a lot from day to day, so that's why we homeschool all year long. —Jammie, North Carolina

On days that I don't have a doctor's appointment or chemo, the kids take turns doing their lessons on the computer. We go to the library at least once a week and the kids will spend some time reading every day. We usually end our school time with lunch and educational television (right now it's Liberty's Kids on Netflix). We also spend at least two days a week on book lessons. Right now we're working on handwriting and memorizing multiplication tables. On doctor or chemo days, we don't change too much. Depending on how late it is or how horrible I feel, we may do a bit less or we do lessons that can be done from the couch. We school year-round, so that gives us a little more leeway with completing our requirements. —Elizabeth, South Carolina

It varies too much for there to be a typical day! Besides regular schoolwork, we also do ballet classes three times a week, swim classes once a week, a co-op class twice a month, and a sign language class once a week. We are also active in our church, attending on Sunday and hosting a small group for other families as well. We plan to have our daughter begin piano lessons again this next school year and art lessons as well. She played soccer the last two years, but we are taking a break from that right now. We are also active in a wonderful Christian homeschool co-op support group, and participate in holiday parties, service projects, field trips, a book club, and more. If you're wondering how we find time to homeschool with all this going on, it can be a challenge. We certainly don't lack opportunities for socialization! —Sandra, California

Part III—Homeschooling Methods

I keep hearing about different homeschooling methods. Which is best?

Homeschooling methods vary widely, depending on the family's schedule, philosophy of learning, and ages of the children. They range from a very structured "school-at-home" approach to a completely unstructured learn-as-you-go "unschooling" approach, with a lot of variation in between.

In general, new homeschoolers tend to start out more structured, then become more relaxed with their methods and materials as they go along. The best method is the one that works well for your family.

In my recent survey of homeschooling families, most of the 344 respondents defined themselves as using one of the seven methods described below. I hope reading about their experiences will help you develop your own approach to homeschooling.

School-at-Home

Families who want a structured method often choose a "school-in-a-box" curriculum. Their days are planned out in advance, typically resembling the public school calendar, and the curriculum usually includes a teacher's guide that tells them exactly what to do every day for each subject.

Many new homeschoolers start out with this method because they feel more comfortable having the guidance it provides. Also, parents of children with special needs (autistic and others) often tell me that using the same routine and resources each day works better for their children than more unstructured methods.

If you decide to start out with an all-in-one curriculum, you can still adjust it to fit your children's needs and learning styles. If a certain part isn't working, either tweak it to make it fit (by reading material aloud, skipping repetitive sections, etc.), or throw it out and find something else.

Your children don't have to do every assignment, complete every worksheet, or take every test. Publishers provide an abundance of material so classroom teachers can choose what they want to use in their classes. They don't know your children, so they can't tailor their materials to their specific needs and interests. But you can, and should. When parents tell me they're burned out, it's usually because they are trying to make their children fit into a one-size-fits-all curriculum, instead of making the curriculum fit their children.

The school-at-home approach is less likely to meet your needs if your children like to follow "rabbit trails" with topics that interest them, or if they don't do well with worksheets and tests. Also, an all-in-one curriculum is more likely to cause frustration for a child who excels in one subject, but is slower in another, since materials cover a single grade level.

In my survey, 9.8% (34 families) identified themselves as using a "textbook, school-at-home" approach. Here are their reasons for choosing this method, and what they like most and least about it:

I like that it is all set up for you. I was not trained as a teacher and I want to make sure I am giving the children a good education. —Cindy, North Carolina

The teacher guides and lesson plans are self-explanatory and coordinate easily with the lessons. It's very methodical and doesn't require a lot of prep work on my end. —Sandy, North Carolina

I am a structure person. I like having everything laid out for me. At first I got really hung up on making sure that I did everything that was planned for the day (checking off the list), but now I am more comfortable with adjusting it based on our needs. —Courtney, North Carolina

With textbooks, the lessons plans are provided. I know that all of the "objectives" are covered, so I don't have to worry if I have covered everything they will need to know. There is little prep time. When we first began and didn't know if we were in it for the long term, I felt it would keep us more on track with where they would be if they were in school and had to go back. What I like least is the quality of the coverage of some subjects, especially science and history. Also, your hands are tied jumping through all the hoops in the book to complete the lesson, leaving little time for expanding on anything.—Lauren, North Carolina

One year we did unschooling. The next school year we went back to textbooks. This is the method that works best for our family because the curriculum is planned out for me. It's easier to make sure everything is covered in the school year. What I least like about this method is feeling like I have to complete the entire book. We also throw in "fun school days" to help with burnout. —Jewel, South Carolina

I like that it's easy to know what to do and to stay organized with several children at once. I don't like that it's not as creative and delight-driven as perhaps Charlotte Mason or unschooling. —Jill, Florida

The textbooks can become boring to the students, but that is when we take spontaneous field trips and life-learning experiences to break things up. We use textbooks, but we don't become legalistic about it. We don't always finish a book, but the textbooks keep us in a pattern of schoolwork.—Sharon, Virginia

Sometimes I get bogged down in the papers that are assigned each day. —Rachel, South Carolina

I like that we get things done and I can see their progress. But I least like the structure and pressure to finish. —Royanne, Ontario, Canada

I most like that someone else puts together the framework, and I just have to do the custom fitting. I don't like that there's no Canadian history, and little world history. —Gwenn, Ontario, Canada

I like it most because I can just follow it, and it's done. What I like least is that it's not creative. —Tabitha, North Carolina

My children are well prepared for a regular classroom (one will take an online class this summer). I dislike the rigidity of the textbooks, but I can do something else to give variety to the day. I assign lots of projects. —Tricia, South Carolina

Online School, Computer-Based Programs

An online school or computer-based approach appeals to families who prefer to have their children answer to someone outside of the family. In my survey, 11 families (3.1%) reported using this method:

We moved to a state that offered the K12 curriculum free through the state. It is well-organized, requiring much less planning time on my part. The curriculum is thorough and challenging enough for my child. —Barbara, Ohio (Author's note: respondent is registered with the public school as a virtual charter school family)

As my children have gotten older, I wanted something they could do on their own and someone else to grade their work. We have been using online schools for the past couple of years. I like that they can be independent from me and I want them to take ownership of their work. I dislike the glitches in the programs and the vagueness of the directions at times. —Gina, Georgia

We started homeschooling in kindergarten and always used A Beka. The first few years we used the traditional curriculum, but last year we switched to A Beka Academy. We are about to finish our second year with it and really like it. —Daniela, South Carolina

We started with textbooks and later used A Beka DVDs as they got older. With the DVDs, I know my students are learning from a qualified teacher in every subject. However, it does take about 6 hours to complete a full day. —Michelle, South Carolina

I like using the virtual academy because they have already pulled together the curriculum. Having a "teacher" as their main source of instruction also takes some of the burden off my shoulders. The children are responsible to me and to an outside entity, which I believe makes them try even harder. It is also another source of support for both the children and me. —Bonnie, Georgia

Classical Homeschooling

Classical homeschoolers believe that children's intellect develops in three stages. During the first stage (generally the elementary years), the focus is on memorizing facts. The next stage (middle school, or when children begin demonstrating abstract reasoning skills), focuses on sorting through the facts to think critically and form accurate conclusions. During the third stage, students (high school, young adult) take all the knowledge they've accumulated and learn to use spoken and written language to express their views.

This method works well for families who enjoy structure, believe in the principles behind a classical education, and don't mind a heavy focus on memorization, reading, and writing. It works less well for families who prefer a more student-directed, flexible approach to learning, or prefer less memorization and a more hands-on, creative method.

In my survey, 33 families (9.5%) described themselves as using this three-stage approach to learning. Here are some of their reasons for choosing the classical method, and what they like most and least:

We were doing preschool with Hands on Homeschooling when my daughter was young. We moved from there to Heart of Dakota. After that, the Lord led us to Classical Conversations. We plan to go through high school with this program. It is phenomenal! —Nicole, Texas

We kept doing what they would do when they went to private school (textbooks and worksheets). We definitely went away from that this year and are much happier with a classical approach, along with literature-based. —LouRae, North Carolina

I started out with a textbook-only approach and then found out about Classical Conversations. I fell in love with it and have been incorporating it into our studies for the past three years. —Elise, South Carolina

I started at home with Sonlight and then our next year we joined a classical homeschool co-op, which was great for us at that time. We stayed in it for five years. Now we are back home again and loving it. The co-op got us connected with other homeschoolers. —Melissa, North Carolina

We were very textbook- and school-oriented in the beginning, but now we use a nice combination of Charlotte Mason and classical. It took a while though. I really had to pay attention to my child's learning style. —Kim, South Carolina

I started with an eclectic approach of textbooks and Charlotte Mason's living books. Now I am using the classical approach because I want my kids to memorize a core body of knowledge. We like that they've memorized a lot of info in all the different subjects, but we miss having more time to read aloud. My daughter has had to do a lot of writing and grammar. She has learned so much, but the process was difficult. We would also like to do more nature studies. Classical education is academically rigorous, but it allows for less flexibility and freedom in the curriculum. I still use living books because they cultivate a love for learning. —Tryphena, Pennsylvania

It took us a few years to figure out what our educational philosophy was. At first, I don't think we had a philosophy, but slowly it became apparent to me that the classical model resonated most closely with my goals for our kids' education. It trains the mind to think logically and connects us with the great minds of the past, but it's easy to get bogged down in having a list of things to complete, and we lose the joy of being together. —Carrie, Illinois

I love that it is designed to teach critical thinking. I also love that my child will begin learning Latin at a young age. —Becky, North Carolina

We enjoy classical education because it is Christ-centered and puts kids on a path for life-long learning. What I like the least is that it's stinking hard and a lot of work! —Deanna, Illinois

I am more involved with my children than I would be if I just handed them workbook pages. However, sometimes more than one child needs me at the same time and the juggling can get frustrating for everyone. We've learned to make allowances for each other. —Mary, North Carolina

I like the classical group of friends that provide social fun for us. I like following a curriculum along with a group so I can discuss it with other families for tips and strategies. I like least that I need to supplement the curriculum with another math program and I feel my child is behind. —Jennifer, Georgia

My kids love it. I believe they can far exceed my expectations learning in this way. I have lots of support. It's easy and doesn't require a lot of expense. I like least that it's a paradigm shift for me, since I was not educated with this methodology. —Molly, North Carolina

I like that it's a tried and true approach. I'm confident my children are getting a solid educational foundation, but sometimes it lacks creativity, so I have to work at getting that in. —Mary, Missouri

I believe the classical method will give my children a good educational foundation. Once they learn to enjoy classical music and literature, they will easily comprehend contemporary subjects. The only con of this method is it takes a lot of time because there is so much memorization, discussion, and writing. —Jiwon, Pennsylvania

The classical method fits our family well. We are assured of rigor, we delight in the exposure our son gets to great ideas and great books, and yet we have enough flexibility to be able to follow rabbit trails. —Libby, Massachusetts

Classical education helps me to make sure that my son has a strong foundation in learning and allows me to learn right along with him. I've never had Latin, so I am learning it at the age of 40. —Dawn, Georgia

Unit Studies

The unit study method focuses on one topic or theme, and incorporates several subjects around that central theme. Students who study weather, for example, will incorporate science (the scientific aspects of weather), history (biggest weather disasters in history), geography (weather patterns around the world), reading/literature (a book about weather), writing (an essay about a weather-related topic, a journal of weather patterns during the duration of the unit study, or a story where weather plays a major role in the plot), and math (temperatures, positive and negative numbers, daily averages).

This approach especially appeals to larger families because all of the children can focus on the same theme, modified to suit different ability levels. They can also use different resources to take advantage of each child's learning style (books for those who learn best by reading, videos for students who are audio/visual learners, experiments and crafts for hands-on learners, and so on.)

Although this method usually results in better retention of material, it's not the first choice for families who want to follow a traditional scope and sequence or are nervous about gaps in learning. It can also be more time-consuming to research and gather resources to suit each student's ability level and learning style.

In my survey, five families (1.4%) identified themselves as using unit studies as their primary approach:

When we first started, I tried a bit of everything (after being overwhelmed at my first homeschool convention vendor hall). For my son, who has special needs, I have found that Amanda Bennett's unit studies are perfect. They are easily adaptable, and cover most of the core curriculum. We can easily revisit units and add to it as he progresses in his ability to understand more complex ideas and material. I would love to be able to use an out-of-the-box curriculum, but with a special needs' child, I have learned that everything needs to be adapted. Out-of-the-box materials are just a lot more work to adapt, for the most part. —Sydney, Michigan

Everything works together. For example, our literature is reading about the historical events we are studying in history, our science goes along with the historical time period, and our language arts is taken from reading and history. —Cathy, Indiana

I like the continuity between subject topics. —Lynne, South Carolina

We can take our time learning about fun and interesting topics. If there is something a child is interested in, I figure I may as well encourage that love of learning. The flexibility is what I like the most. —Michelle, Pennsylvania

Charlotte Mason, Living Books, & Literature-Based Methods

These approaches focus on using good literature (classics, biographies, historical fiction, etc.) instead of textbooks as a main resource. They also emphasize short lessons for academic subjects, narration (verbally repeating learned material) to solidify knowledge, nature studies, and the study of fine arts (music, art, crafts).

They work well for students who are strong readers, enjoy audio books, or who have parents who read aloud to them. They don't work as well for students who have difficulty reading or processing auditory information.

In my survey, 23 families (6.6%) described themselves as using a literature-based approach to learning. Many shared their experiences with this method:

I started out "safe" with A Beka and Bob Jones, but quickly moved into unit studies. I finally settled on Charlotte Mason. This is much more enjoyable for all, and they are developing a deeper level of knowledge. However, I don't have enough time to read all the books my older children do, so it makes it hard to have a good discussion about them. —Nancy, North Carolina

I started out with textbooks (school-at-home). I soon learned that textbooks didn't fit my teaching style, or my kids' learning styles. I have changed curriculum every year until this year. This is the first year I have been happy with the choices I've made. We get to learn from great literature, instead of boring textbooks. My children actually enjoy school now instead of just enduring it. —Allison, South Carolina

We started out more classical, based on the method described in Susan Wise Bauer's The Well-Trained Mind, but have shifted more into Charlotte Mason. I love the sweet fellowship we share while reading together on the couch, but we are still rigorous with math and science. I like the literature methods, including narration, dictation, and copywork. They are working very well for my children. I love the nature studies. —Julia, South Carolina

We began with textbooks and workbooks, but disliked the similarity to public school. So we switched to using Charlotte Mason. It has been so much more relaxed in our home since we made the change. I love the amount of literature my daughter is exposed to and the discussions we have. My least favorite part is trying to fit in all the subjects I'm not used to doing, such as nature study and art appreciation. But I'm not giving up! —Lara, South Carolina

In the beginning of my homeschool journey, I thought homeschooling was supposed to be "classroom" school at home. My daughter was frustrated with learning and I was exhausted trying to duplicate something I didn't even enjoy as a child. After much prayer and advice from a seasoned homeschooler, I started over. We began going on nature walks every day, cooked something (big or small) each day, read tons of books together, and I focused more on enjoying my children and helping them love learning! I love that my children are learning, but do not think of it as "school." They do their own math and reading each day, but we do science and history together, using real living books, lots of reading, videos, and visiting these places firsthand. They tell all of their friends that they only have to do math and reading because they think that all the other learning they do is not "school." I love that, but with three children, sometimes it's hard to make sure they're all getting something from what we are reading. —Brooke, South Carolina

I love that the Charlotte Mason method is gentle and allows for flexibility based on the family and child. —Victoria, South Carolina

I'm a big fan of the literature-based method. Textbooks are boring! I personally enjoy the curriculum as we work through it. I'm learning, too, even with my first-grader. —Tiffany, Mississippi

We use books to read aloud, lap-booking, and note-booking. Both of my sons are ADD/ADHD, so we use books they are interested in and they learn better that way. I love the Charlotte Mason way of teaching. —Robyn, Georgia

Unschooling, Relaxed, & Child-Led Methods

With unschooling, relaxed, and child-led approaches, students direct their own education. They decide what they want to learn and how they want to learn it, while parents provide resources and guidance, as needed. Students tend to learn topics quickly and in more depth because they're self-motivated and deeply engaged in their own learning.

This method works best for families who are comfortable without a scope and sequence, or any other pre-determined plan. It's less successful for parents who prefer structure, or have concerns about letting their children set the pace and choose their own topics. It can also be more time-intensive for parents because they have to research and gather resources whenever their children's interests or needs change.

In my survey, 17 families (4.9%) identified themselves as using one of these more relaxed approaches:

We're much more relaxed now; less "school at home," because that is not how children learn best. I like the hands-on experiences and the children don't dread learning because it is fun to them. They get to choose what they want to learn about so they are less resistant. —Crystal, Maryland

As an unschooling family, we've occasionally decided the kids needed to do more bookwork. After a few weeks, we realize they're missing out on some real in-depth experiences and wasting time on schoolish busywork. I like them to have the opportunity to follow interests and spend unlimited time on areas of interest, but there is a lack of social support and understanding of our lives. People we know will talk disparagingly about families like us, without knowing we follow the same style. —Diane, New Mexico

When I first started homeschooling, I was very rigid and did my best to duplicate the county curriculum. I learned very quickly that my kids are like sponges, and will absorb information very quickly and easily if I let them follow their own interests. They've learned more about ancient and current Egypt, the European Middle Ages, and physics than most adults. I think I've made learning fun again. Public school seems to be mainly concerned with making sure the kids pass tests. They don't care if students really understand the information, they just want them to know the answers and be able to regurgitate them on cue. My kids are creative and inquisitive, and I allow them to be as creative and inquisitive as they want to be. They end up taking learning journeys they'd never have bothered with when I was spoonfeeding them boring facts to memorize. —Jamy, North Carolina

We started off with a packaged curriculum, which was frustrating and too much like "school" for our liking. We gradually became less structured and eventually took the plunge into full blown "unschooling." It's so exciting to see my daughter passionately pursuing learning in her interest areas. It is an amazing process to be a part of! Unfortunately, society, in general, has such a negative view of our type of homeschooling. It is viewed as "doing nothing" and "lazy parenting," when in reality, it takes a great deal of parental involvement and keeps us much busier than when we were doing the curriculum. —Pam, Illinois

I started our homeschooling experience with table work: papers, reading books, and games. We had a routine. Now we do things when we are in the mood. We go for walks, play Legos, go on field trips, watch videos, and so on. If the kids show an interest in something, I try to give them as much information as they want. —Kathy, South Carolina

There have been times through the years when I've questioned myself. So I go out and buy curricula, thinking we need to revamp our whole approach. That has never survived a month. We always revert back to child-led learning in a very "unschooly" way. My kids are very bright and pursue a wide variety of interests. I love, love, love that. I don't like the inevitable boredom that comes without a specific structure, but it always leads to creativity, if we just ride it out long enough. I don't like feeling like I'm not doing enough, but I think that happens no matter what method you follow. —Caroline, North Carolina

I like the relaxed method. I enjoy teaching my children subjects they are interested in and not what some group of adults thinks my child would like. The unschooling method works for us due to the varied ages and busy lifestyles of our children. My only absolute requirements are reading, writing and math. Those subjects are not up for discussion—they are a must. I sometimes worry that my oldest child is falling behind the "norm" due to our unschooling and relaxed method. My fears are probably irrational and unnecessary, but I still worry. —Rebecca, Michigan

I love that we are free to learn what we want, when we want. The girls choose what they want to learn and enjoy it a lot more than when they were in public school. The only downside is that I have to do a little more research on a topic, and find crafts or games that might go along with each day's topic. But I also love this process and would probably do it anyway. Every morning I look at different websites and find stuff we can do that day. No day is the same! —Chrissie, Georgia

We enjoy having the freedom to cover topics as long as we want, and choose those topics ourselves. But sometimes it is difficult to keep on task since we aren't following one program. —Pamela, Ohio

I love that my kids are mostly free to choose what they learn and, as a result, are intrinsically motivated. It's amazing to see how much more they have learned since leaving public school than they ever did there. Even in the traditional academic areas, they seem to have acquired knowledge just by living their lives and following their interests without ever having a formal lesson. What I like least is the fact that so many other families have bought into the public school's way of teaching and learning. It can be hard sometimes to go against what we've all been conditioned for decades (centuries, really) to think is the only way to be educated. Those learning and teaching in a traditional manner seem to have a hard time understanding and accepting unschooling. —Janice, North Carolina

This method follows my child's lead and allows him to pursue his interests to whatever depth he desires. I feel this allows the best chance for comprehension and retention of the material. He is allowed to excel in areas where he has strengths, without difficult areas holding him back. That doesn't mean we don't address the areas where he struggles. We weave learning into everyday life. Every day is a "school" day. We are always learning, and we are learning together. We love it! —Wendy, Virginia

Eclectic (Mix & Match) Method

While most new homeschoolers start out with a specific plan (usually one of the methods previously described), the vast majority find themselves making changes as they go along. In my survey, the majority of families (208, 60.4%) settled into an eclectic approach. Instead of using a single method, they use a variety based on the needs of their children and the subject being taught. Here are some of the reasons they ended up choosing this mix-and-match approach:

At first I didn't want to stray too far from what I thought was proper, so I stuck to textbooks and followed a regimented schedule like public school. Eventually I figured out I had freedom to tailor my children's education to fit their individual needs, strengths, and interests. I added videos, television, the library, homeschooling group classes, etc. My sons are not only educated, but now they've learned how to learn. —Susan, Michigan

We started out very classical and workbook-based, then moved to a more Charlotte Mason-style with lots of living books. As we enter the high school years, the kids are independent learners. They help plan their courses and dig in daily because it interests them. —Denise, North Carolina

We began five years ago doing school-at-home (it was all I knew!), and we forgot the real reasons why we educate at home. We now have fun (most of the time) engaging in studies and activities that the children are most interested in, or I find a way to incorporate what I want them to learn into a way that seems more engaging for them. —Diana, Ontario, Canada

When I first began homeschooling, I tried to do school-at-home. However, my children made me see that school was so much more than just sitting inside doing bookwork. Over the years I have let them design their own course of study and let them choose or design their own curriculum. —Kathye, North Carolina

Originally, I used a boxed curriculum because I thought it was my only option. I let fear of messing up rule my decisions. Once I became more confident in our journey, I changed to a more eclectic method. I didn't like feeling we were just going through the motions. I didn't feel like we were accomplishing many of the goals we had when we began homeschooling. My children were bored with workbooks and weren't retaining the information or enjoying learning. —Kellie, Kentucky

With my eldest three children, I used textbooks because I was a single mom and needed the "easiest" route. Once I adopted younger children, I did more searching and found that teaching a strong foundation in the "three R's" was primary to all other academic growth. So we moved to teaching as a family unit for all other subjects, with much more literature, hands-on learning, notebooking, field trips, and nature studies to develop a delight in our home for learning. —Lisa, Delaware

We started out very strict with a schedule and tons of lessons to accomplish. I had tests and quizzes planned for every subject. My daughter was stressed with all the things to do, just like when she was in school, and that is one of the reasons I pulled her out. We are now very relaxed. We learn the "three R's" and study history through historical fiction, biographies, videos, field trips, etc. No tests! With all the one-on-one interaction, I know what they get and what they need help with. —Sheri, South Carolina

I originally began thinking I would be a die-hard Classical homeschooler. I read The Well-Trained Mind by Susan Wise Bauer, and it fully resonated with me. However, my son had issues with attention and it made it difficult to follow that method. We were both ending the days feeling stressed and defeated. He began to hate school and learning, so I knew I needed to change things quickly. We now use more of a Charlotte Mason method overall, especially for literature, history, and science. We are all much happier now! —Jennifer, North Carolina

I started out always by the book. We were behaving more like a public school at home, but now I don't stress about things like I used to. The kids are more involved in the things they want to learn. We complete a lot of lapbooks and read, read, read everything. —Monica, South Carolina

We began with A Beka DVD schooling and have moved to a more Charlotte Mason, living books, literature-based learning, although I do try to base it on the individual child. We still use outside classes sometimes. I like the flexibility of determining what we learn each day and don't like to be in a "box." I love relaxed homeschooling and instilling a love of learning rather than drudgery. —Julie, Georgia

We changed from unschooling to a more eclectic mix because of my son's Aspergers. Providing more structure worked better for him. —Amy, North Carolina

When I first started homeschooling, I was worried about checking every box and making sure that my daughter was doing the same things public school children were doing. Over the years, I have become more relaxed. We focus on logic, interest-based learning, and really enjoying learning. With that said, I am still rigid with math. I feel like I have to be—you can't get through life without it. —Tracy, Georgia

What I thought would work and interest the kids did not. As the kids have gotten older, I involve them more in choosing subjects and methods (books, videos, and computer). I actually spend less money now on curriculum due to their choices and the abundant information online and through networks like PBS (wonderful archives), Discovery Channel, and History Channel —Jan, South Carolina

We used textbook and units the first year, a more relaxed Charlotte Mason-style the second year, and were eclectic with some unschooling for the third and fourth years. If I had understood what unschooling really was, I would have been unschooling from the beginning! —Deb, South Carolina

I began as a classical homeschooler, but soon learned that having child-led learning was much more fulfilling for everyone. (We still use a curriculum for math, grammar, and handwriting.) It is a lot less work for me, other than driving to the library countless times, and much more memorable for them. —Sonya, Maine

I began homeschooling with textbooks and quickly learned that hands-on learning with smaller unit studies worked best for us. We will always use the Teaching Textbooks computer program for math, though. It's been a blessing for us. —Kim, South Carolina

We came from public school, so at first we were very traditional in our learning (worksheets, etc.). Now we are more laid back and use living books for learning. (For math and science, we are still pretty much by the book.) We are focusing on other things besides academics—character! We aren't focused so much on learning facts as we are learning life lessons. —Alana, North Carolina

We started with a virtual school because I was clueless about what to buy and where to begin. After the first year, we ditched the virtual school and went our own way. I was much more comfortable with choosing curriculum and we were tired of the state hoops we had to jump through. The virtual school was too structured for us. We are a little bit unschooling, a little bit classical method. We're laid back, but my son still likes workbooks. —Christina, Ohio

I learned to relax and be led more by my children's interests. I realized it was okay to drop a curriculum if it wasn't working out (even if it was expensive!). I learned the most important thing was not a specific checklist of acquired skills, but for me to inspire them to love learning and become self-motivated. As my children have grown, I've become less teacher and more coordinator, facilitator, and chauffeur. —Kerstin, New Jersey

Drawbacks of the Eclectic Method

Although the freedom and flexibility of the eclectic approach is its biggest strength, there are some drawbacks. Here's what my survey families had to say:

I least like the uncertainty that comes with going your own way instead of the assurance of following a tried-and-true curriculum. —Sandi, North Carolina

I don't like that I can't do it again with all the newer, more exciting things available now! There was never enough time to teach all I wanted to. —Chris, Virginia

It takes time to figure everything out and it might be easier if a complete packaged curriculum did it all. —Zoe, South Carolina

I have to do a lot of research, be proactive and involved. It takes a lot of time and energy to do that. —Aubyn, Ontario, Canada

What I like least is all the research I have to do every year around this time (spring and summer). I am always happy with the end result, but spend many hours trying to figure it all out. —Jennifer, Michigan

I still occasionally feel anxiety when I realize my children may not be studying some of the things public school children are learning. (I forget the great things they *are* learning.) I also seem not to have enough time in the day to do everything. —Diana, Ontario, Canada

It's hard to measure whether we are done with a subject or not. It requires a lot of pre-planning on my part, because if I don't have it planned in advance, it's easy to get so busy with activities that school gets put by the wayside by December. And now that my daughter is a junior, I'm finding it difficult to write an acceptable NCAA transcript because I have relied on a lot of websites for my curriculum. They prefer "canned" textbooks with a table of contents. —Kathye, North Carolina

I do worry sometimes that I might not be covering all the bases, so I use a scope and sequence to determine where they might have any weaknesses and we work on them. —Kellie, Kentucky

What I like least is trying to grade the work. Since we are not traditional, it is hard to assign a grade for a subject. I try to be as objective as possible and am thankful that at this stage in my son's education, a pass/fail is all the grading I need to do. My daughter's grades will be assigned letters and not percentages. —Sheri, South Carolina

The drawbacks of this method are the time and research I put into choosing the different curricula, although I do often use the same materials for a subject if it is working well. Ordering from different companies can cost extra for shipping, and sometimes it's more teacher-intensive to learn how to teach each subject when the resources come from different companies. —Donna, Georgia

I am not so organized with the eclectic method. It is hard to be organized when you go off on a different path during the middle of a lesson because they have shown interest or asked a question. —Terri, Tennessee

Sometimes I crave more structure for myself, and feel less organized than when we use textbooks —Rose, South Carolina

I have a tendency to be a "box checker," so it is hard sometimes to relax and take learning at our pace instead of the curriculum's pace. However, now that my children are older, I am seeing the fruits of my labor. —Kim, Georgia

I have to work really hard to stay organized. I am actually considering a more structured curriculum for my son because I think he needs it. But my daughter has done quite well with my 'free form' method. —Tracy, Georgia

The hardest part with the eclectic method is fitting everything together so it flows and accomplishes the results I am looking for! Staying alert to what is not working for a child, and changing even if I prefer the original choice, is probably my least favorite thing. —Linda, Georgia

What I like least is just a carryover of my traditional school experience—we jump around a lot in history and science, studying specific periods and topics in depth instead of covering things chronologically and very broadly like schools do. Even now, I worry I will miss something they might need. —Jan, South Carolina

It is a bit harder to make curriculum decisions (even though it is more fun) than purchasing an "out-of-the-box" curriculum —Jackie, Georgia

Using an eclectic approach is a bit more cumbersome for me, as the teacher/mom, because it requires me to research all the materials available for each subject. I have to be more hands-on with our school, too. We have only one child, but I can see how it would be harder for someone with more children. However, the benefits of teaching to our son's strengths have been priceless. —Janet, South Carolina

Freedom and variety is the best thing about being eclectic, but it goes hand in hand with what I like the least, which is the lack of structure. We are still working on finding a happy medium. —Risa, South Carolina

I worry about whether the boys are learning everything they need, but when I have them tested, they both score well above average, so we are happy with the results. —Sheila, Tennessee

There is more hands-on work and less free time for me with this method. With a complete curriculum, I would be able to supervise my son's work and spend less time one-on-one. I spend more time looking for resources than I would with a packaged curriculum, but I enjoy it. —Christina, Ohio

I worry about the topics not overlapping, leaving gaps in their knowledge. For example, when we study history, we read living history books. I worry I will not cover everything since I do not buy a complete curriculum. However, I know that they can research anything I missed. —Shelley, Texas

I sometimes feel stressed because I wonder if we're doing enough and if she's really learning what she needs to be. Will there be "holes?" —Sandra, California

Attempting to meet the needs of each child can be overwhelming because all of my children learn best with different methods. —Erin, South Carolina

Part IV—Curriculum & Resources

How do I choose a curriculum?

The sheer volume of products marketed to homeschoolers these days can be overwhelming. To help you choose, I asked families from my online community to share their "one favorite homeschool resource" and explain why it was their favorite. Although this list is very limited, I hope their answers will serve as a springboard for you to begin choosing your own materials.

Audiobooks and Magazines

Ask, Muse, Odyssey, Cobblestone, Cricket, and other Carus Publishing Magazines
800.821.0115
www.cricketmag.com/home.asp
In over 20 years of homeschooling, these magazines are the one resource that's stayed with us throughout. My children devour these excellent science, history, social studies, and literary magazines, month after month. They've commented many times on history or science topics, and when asked where they learned their information, they almost always reply, "Oh, I read it in Muse (or Odyssey, or Ask, or Click, or Appleseeds…)." The articles are well-written and engaging, and the content is more current and relevant than what's found in many textbooks. They often include more recent scientific and historical discoveries. They tend to run a little older than their age guidelines, in my opinion, so I recommend requesting sample issues (or reviewing them at

your local library) before choosing which to subscribe to. Their rates are higher than other magazines because there isn't any advertising. I love the lack of ads, though, and they're totally worth the price. If you get multiple subscriptions, you can usually get significant discounts, so make sure to ask. —Dianna, South Carolina

Boomerang! Children's Audio Magazine
800.333.7858
www.boomkids.com
While we use other resources along with Boomerang now, there was a time when this was practically our "one and only." We listen to these audio magazines repeatedly, learning and retaining information about the lives of interesting and important people from the past and present. There are also stories about travel, cooking, and humanity—with some jokes tossed around. Good, good stuff! —Deanna, Tennessee

Jim Weiss Audio Books
(Available via Amazon.com and other bookstores)
Jim Weiss' stories have captivated all of us. We love to listen to them over and over again. They make history and science very real to my children. An added bonus is the rich vocabulary I hear repeated in my home. They are awesome! —Heather, Virginia

Educational Websites, Videos, and Streaming

BrainPOP and BrainPOP Jr.
www.brainpop.com and www.brainpopjr.com
These websites have a wealth of educational and entertaining videos that help me feel like I'm adding that last "ah-ha!" after I've covered a subject. My children are in

3rd and 4th grades, and it's a great way to lightly review a topic with a different perspective and voice. We love them! —Sandi, North Carolina

Discovery Education Streaming Plus
www.discoveryeducation.com
We use this for Elementary Spanish and for accessing videos for every subject. —Anne, Massachusetts

Google
www.google.com
My favorite teaching resource is Google's search engine. When the kids have questions about science or history, I search the topic on Google and we have an answer in minutes. —Kathleen, Maryland

Khan Academy
www.khanacademy.org
He is so cool; smart and informative! —Betsy, North Carolina. The best freebie has been Kahn academy's math, from kindergarten to quantum physics. —Danny, North Carolina

Time4Learning
www.time4learning.com
Although both of my boys have now passed the age when they can use Time4Learning (it only goes up through 8th grade), it is definitely the single best resource we ever discovered for homeschooling. The lessons are comprehensive and engaging, and the program is user-friendly. For visual learners, the multimedia format is spot on! It was the best homeschool resource we encountered during twelve years of homeschooling. —Kerry, North Carolina

Math Resources

Math-U-See
888.854.6284

www.mathusee.com

Math-U-See is my favorite math series. It takes us step-by-step through all levels of math, building on each level in a way that is easy for my children to understand. I finally understand things I didn't get before. My children love it!
—Linda, South Carolina

RightStart Mathematics
888.775.6284

rightstartmath.com

This curriculum has taken away all my stress of teaching math to my daughter. She looks forward to math and we enjoy it together. She's testing way above grade level with no struggle, just joyous learning. —Amy, North Carolina

Teaching Textbooks
866.867.6284

www.teachingtextbooks.com

Math has always been easy for me, but not for my children. No matter how hard I tried to hide my frustration when they were struggling with a concept, they could sense it and this made it more frustrating for them. They didn't understand the math, and felt inadequate and "dumb" because they couldn't get it. Teaching Textbooks removes me from the picture altogether and allows them to stop worrying about pleasing me and just focus on learning the math. —Sarah, North Carolina

Life of Fred Mathematics

800.653.4231

www.lifeoffredmath.com

I decided to take a break from a regular math curriculum to try Life of Fred. I thought it would be just a temporary diversion, but it turned out that my kids loved it and were really learning math. They flew through fractions, decimals, percent, and pre-algebra. They are now doing beginning algebra. I was amazed that a math curriculum written in a story format could really teach math. —Kim, Ohio

An abacus

An abacus is my favorite resource. It can be used with math students throughout their elementary years, and it's small for storage. Students work quicker with it since they aren't hunting for pieces, lining them up, flipping them over, stacking them, nor are they distracted creating imaginative playthings. The pieces don't get lost. Its smooth movement attracts students and makes math just a bit more exciting. It can be utilized regardless of which curriculum a student is comfortable with. It's fun and efficient! —Jennifer, North Carolina

History Resources

Story of the World

877.322.3445

www.welltrainedmind.com/store

Story of the World has been a great history series for us. I really like the way history is presented chronologically and in small bits with corresponding literature suggestions and extra activities. —Amy, Georgia

Beautiful Feet Books
800.889.1978
www.bfbooks.com
I loved Beautiful Feet history for high school with our son, who is now 19. —Cynthia, North Carolina

America the Beautiful by Notgrass
800.211.8793
www.notgrass.com
This is my favorite for history. The chronological layout is wonderful. The timeline and maps let you see where and when events happened as you learn about history and the people involved. The accompanying textbook, We the People, adds depth and warmth. The people my children learn about become more real, and history becomes more about the people, and how one event led to another. It definitely brings history to life and is perfect for middle school students. —Tara, Tennessee

Science Resources

Apologia Science
888.524.4724
www.apologia.com/prodas.php
My favorites are the Apologia Science books: General Science, Physical Science, Biology, and Chemistry. They're well-written, very instructive, and prepare the student for college science. —Betty, South Carolina

Handbook of Nature Study
Anna Comstock's Handbook of Nature Study is my favorite resource. We do lots of nature studies as part of our daily schooling, and this resource is so comprehensive, it is really all we need. You can do a complete science lesson with this

book, or just use it as a field guide to look something up. I've used it for science, history, and language arts. Even though we have shelves full of books and field guides, this is my go-to resource. —Anne, South Carolina

Supercharged Science
www.superchargedscience.com
My favorite resource is Supercharged Science. My daughter is difficult to homeschool. Her attention span is short and her motivation is somewhat hampered. This website is easy for me to understand and very hands-on, so it keeps her interested. I have used it for the better part of two years, and will continue to use it. —Cendi, Colorado

Language Arts Resources

Excellence in Writing
800.856.5815
www.excellenceinwriting.com
This has been one of my favorite resources to teach writing. It takes out the guesswork for me and gives very specific rules for the student to follow. It slowly builds writing skills, starting with outlines and note-taking. This program also helps point out where to find the most important information in a text. —Stephanie, South Carolina

Handwriting Without Tears
301.263.2700
www.hwtears.com/hwt
This is our favorite. It has a quick, easy-to-complete lesson for each day, and the transition from print to cursive is simple to follow. —Carmen, South Carolina

McGuffey's Eclectic Primer

by William Holmes McGuffey

I highly recommend this for children starting to read or who are struggling with reading. It has been revised, but the original came out in 1881. The method is simple, but it helps make reading "click" for young children. My mother and grandparents learned to read from this book, too, which shows me it's a definite winner. My five-year-old son can read very well now, and we haven't even gotten through the whole book. —Becky, North Carolina

Teaching Your Child to Read in 100 Easy Lessons

by Siegfried Engelmann, Phyllis Haddox, and Elaine Bruner

This is my favorite because it worked for all of my children, even though each has different learning abilities and styles. It's scripted, and has short lessons, so it's easy for mom and child. —Janey, South Carolina

Total Language Plus

360.754.3660

site.totallanguageplus.com

This is my favorite for language arts because it lays out the lesson plan for you. Spelling, vocabulary, and grammar are integrated with books the students read, and there is a fabulous list of ideas to choose from to help enrich and reinforce the learning. —Tara, Tennessee

Multi-Subject Resources

Amanda Bennet Download N Go

832.387.6646

www.unitstudy.com/downloadngo.html

We love Amanda Bennett Download N Go unit studies. We print them out and bind them in a report cover, but also follow along on the computer because there are links embedded in the unit study. My son learns research, navigation, and typing skills as we go! —Sydney, Michigan

Heart of Dakota
605.428.4068
www.heartofdakota.com
Heart of Dakota is my favorite resource for a Charlotte Mason-style education. I have tried so many different things, and none of them were as easy to implement or as fun for my children. —Allison, South Carolina

My Father's World
573.202.2000
www.mfwbooks.com
This covers so much material and is fun and entertaining. I learn a lot, and so do the children. And it is Christ-centered. —Juli, Georgia

Sonlight
303.730.6292
www.sonlight.com
Sonlight curriculum is my absolute favorite resource. Everything is literature-based. Children read books (not textbooks) and look at pictures and they learn! I knew it was for us the first year I used it. My kids would ask me if they could read "just one more book" even after we finished with school for the day. Now, three years later, I have four children who have a love for reading and learning. Whenever they are interested in something, they ask me to find books about the topic. When it is time for school to start they have their books out and are waiting on me. It's great! —Jessie, South Carolina

Unit Studies Made Easy

813-758-6793

http://www.valeriebendt.com

This book has opened up a whole new world of learning for us. Before reading it, I was too scared to venture away from the standard boxed curriculum. I worried that my kids might miss out on something important. It showed me how to incorporate everything so I can be confident I'm covering everything my state requires. It showed me how to make learning a fun adventure for all of us. —Kellie, Kentucky

School-in-a-Box and Correspondence Schools

A Beka DVDs

877.223.5226

www.abeka.com

My son and I have been using the A Beka DVD program since the 3rd grade (we are now going into 9th) and I love it. It has worked well for us, but I will admit it is not for everyone. —Jennifer, South Carolina

Calvert School

888.487.4652

homeschool.calvertschool.org

I use Calvert School and love it. I subscribed to the Additional Teaching Service as well. I can't say that having the Certified Teacher makes that much of a difference, but I do like that I have an official transcript and a certificate of completion. —Courtney, North Carolina

K12

866.512.6463

www.k12.com

I like this because it has a high level of academic information, a variety of activities, and different ways of presenting the material. I can customize it to meet the needs of our family, as well as the educational needs and pace of each child. —Kimberly, North Carolina

Mother of Divine Grace

805.646.5818

www.motherofdivinegrace.org

My correspondence school, Mother of Divine Grace, has been my favorite resource. I am in charge of the curriculum, grading, correcting, etc., but they keep the records and provide the documentation for high school transcripts. I also have a consultant who helps me with learning difficulties. The suggestions and support I have received from that one person, my consultant, is worth the "price of admission." —Mary Kate, North Carolina

Seton Home Study School

540.636.9990

www.setonhome.org

After shopping around and using different curricula, we ended up with Seton Home Study School. It is a Catholic curriculum, which is important to us. When you enroll your children, you have access to counselors, online resources, as well as a staff who actually answer their phones. Their cost is quite low compared to others. They are accredited, which may be helpful for some parents as their children reach high school. Some tests are sent out to be graded by their graders, while others are graded by the parent. Overall, we are extremely pleased with the quality, amount of work assigned, and the ease of speaking with a counselor when we need help. —Rosemarie, South Carolina

Switched on Schoolhouse
800.622.3070
www.aophomeschooling.com/switched-on-schoolhouse
I like this because it covers all my state's standards, and it's easy to add other topics. It generates report cards and assists with grading. It's perfect for me because I work full-time. —Debi, Utah

Books About Homeschooling

Educating the WholeHearted Child
by Clay Clarkson with Sally Clarkson
This book addresses all areas of education: academic, emotional, and spiritual. I appreciate the authors' focus on developmental appropriateness of materials and the goal of establishing an enriching environment for children. —Ann, North Carolina

I Saw the Angel in the Marble
by Chris and Ellyn Davis
Chris and Ellyn Davis were homeschool pioneers and this book is a collection of their newsletters (in the days before the internet). I often go back and read these articles to remind myself why I homeschool. I began because I knew traditional schooling wasn't the best way for my children, especially my son, to learn. However, it is easy to get sucked into the school-at-home syndrome instead of making education a part of everyday life. Whenever I start to doubt my ability to educate my kids or fall into the "we're behind" trap, I revisit this book. It keeps me focused on why and how to really homeschool. —Kathye, North Carolina

The Ultimate Guide to Homeschooling
by Debra Bell
As a newbie, this gave me fabulous information about resources and tons of options to look into. It's definitely the right combination of God-centered wisdom, yet not too preachy. —Susan, South Carolina

Curriculum Reviews & Homeschool Helps

Cathy Duffy Reviews
www.cathyduffyreviews.com
As a new homeschooler, my favorite resource was the Cathy Duffy review website. Her book 100 Top Picks for Homeschool Curriculum was the first one I read on the subject. It was an excellent starting point, not only for specific curricula, but also for each family's preferred teaching method and each child's learning style. I highly recommend it! —Jennifer, South Carolina

EdHelper.com
www.edhelper.com
This is the educational resource I've used most since I started homeschooling. I've used it over the years for supplemental materials for math, grammar, and "on this day" celebrations. My favorite part is the literature unit. You can find a book and there is everything you can imagine to go along with the unit. —Pam, North Carolina

HomeSchool Reviews
www.homeschoolreviews.com
This is a great place to find out what other moms think of a curriculum. It has been such a huge help to me over the years! —Tracy, North Carolina

Homeschool Tracker

www.homeschooltracker.com

My daily must-have is Homeschool Tracker software. I use it to keep track of what we do and when, including field trips. It allows me to create our library just by typing in a book's ISBN, and it needs only a one-click check-mark for each assignment completed (once the subjects and courses are set up). It even generates progress reports. —Jennifer, South Carolina

Well-Trained Mind Forums

www.welltrainedmind.com/forums

I can find tons of information about homeschooling at the Well-Trained Mind forums while interacting online with other homeschoolers around the world. I have learned a great deal about curricula, teaching and learning styles, organization, dealing with behaviors and those difficult days, co-op ideas, crafts, different reasons for homeschooling, and the variety of ways to approach it. I could go on and on. The men and women on this board are dedicated to homeschooling, and they are openly willing to share their experiences, trials and triumphs, and more. Although it was created around the classical model described in Susan Wise Bauer's book, The Well-Trained Mind, the variety of homeschoolers in this forum is incredible. Everyone is seeking the same goal of doing what is best for their family, and they all strive to do it the best way they can. —Jennifer, North Carolina

The Workbox System

www.workboxsystem.com

This is a system that helps you get organized with just about any curriculum. I am not the most organized person, and this is a simple and comprehensive method to get me started on my year, and keep me going. It made it very easy for me to make and set goals for completing the school work for the year. And my kids loved the sense of accomplishment and independence that the system provides. —Stacy, North Carolina

Places, People, and Miscellaneous

Public Libraries

My public library is my favorite resource. It offers so much: regular books; books on CD (which we listen to religiously in the car); digital audiobooks you can download at home and listen to on an MP3 player; e-books you can read on Kindles, Nooks, and other devices; DVDs; and magazines. They show movies, have summer reading programs, and let us use rooms for our Lego club, book club, and chess club. And my daughter even dissected something there (a sheep heart, I think). It's an amazingly versatile resource! —Zoe, South Carolina

Local Homeschool Groups

My favorite resource is my local homeschool group. They always give me tips, ideas, activities, and support. —Pam, North Carolina

Academic Groups

Our Classical Conversations group has helped our homeschool come together and have direction. It has blessed us with community and curriculum that is challenging. The children and I have learned a lot and I see the fruits of a classical education. —Fanesta, Illinois

Yahoo Groups

I love to look through catalogs and see the wonderful products out there, but my favorite resource is our homeschool yahoo group. There's nothing like getting personal recommendations from people who have used different materials. I've been introduced to amazing resources through our group. It is always my number one go-to when I am looking for something. —Natalie, Florida

Field Trips, Projects, Group Activities

We like hands-on resources such as field trips, internet, libraries, Girl Scouts, 4-H, church-sponsored activities, volunteer projects, museums, concerts, and plays. We also use state, national, and local parks and recreation services. Other sources would include the Department of Natural Resources and various other educational government agencies. —Denise, South Carolina

Multiple Resources

My favorite resources are things I can introduce to my kids, which they may then choose to pursue. Some examples are Khan Academy, BrainPop, GameGoo, Wikipedia, and many more. I also love, love, love audiobooks. The kids and I listen to them whenever we're all in the car together, which is often. We get them from the public library for free. We stream a lot of video from Netflix, Amazon, and Nova. I check out bunches of nonfiction books from the library and strew them around the house. I get ones which are on subjects of current interest as well as ones which I think may be a possible new interest. We spend a lot of time at the library. —Janice, North Carolina

Publishers and Catalogs

Christianbook.com
800.247.4784

www.christianbook.com

Nine times out of ten, I can look through the book I'm considering at the Christianbook.com website. Since I can browse a sample online, I don't have to order and send it back if I don't like it, or wait to ask someone to let me look through their copy before buying my own. —Kim, South Carolina

CurrClick
www.currclick.com

CurrClick is a one-stop kind of shopping place. Everything is there, and it always has a lot of freebies. —Wilda, Tennessee

Homeschool Buyers Co-op
www.homeschoolbuyersco-op.org

The Homeschool Buyers Co-op is my favorite website, and I check it daily. They get great group buys on curriculum and offer ID cards, which are worth more to us than any other resource. We have gotten discounts at bookstores, attractions, and parks with our cards. I couldn't homeschool without them! —Erin, South Carolina

Rainbow Resource Catalog
888.841.3456

www.rainbowresource.com

The Rainbow Resource catalog is the size of a large phone book, with extensive reviews of thousands of products. It's helped us in our curriculum choices over the years. When one of our resources is not working, browsing through their catalog and the reviews has helped turn our course in a different direction. —Jenny, Texas

Veritas Press
800.922.5082
www.veritaspress.com
Veritas Press has excellent products, great prices, and spiritual content to their materials. —Royce, South Carolina

I hope you've enjoyed reading about the resources my survey families consider to be their favorites. Visit the links area of my website at carolinahomeschooler.com/alinks.html to see more popular choices, including free lending libraries, reading reward programs, book lists, videos, worksheets, samples, lesson plans, interactive websites, and more.

Before you purchase anything, try to see materials first-hand at a convention, book fair, or through members of your local support group. Homeschool families are often very willing to show you what has worked for them (and what hasn't). If you can't find a copy to review, look for samples at the company's website, or call them and ask if they can send samples via regular mail.

Whatever you choose to start out with, keep it simple until you learn what best fits your children's learning styles. You can always make adjustments as you go along.

You're also welcome to join our Facebook community and Yahoo group to ask other parents about curriculum and learning styles (see www.carolinahomeschooler.com/acommunity.html for links to all of our community areas).

Part V—The High School Years

What about high school?

High school usually requires more documentation than the earlier grades, but it's manageable. If your student plans to attend college and compete for scholarships, you'll need to keep track of grades and credits for his transcript beginning in the 9th grade. If he plans to enter the workforce or start his own business after graduation, you'll need to focus more on increasing practical living and career skills. Both paths are discussed in more depth in the following sections.

How many classes should my student take?

Plan for six to eight credits each year (24 to 32 total), where each full course (150-180 hours) earns one credit, and each semester course (75-90 hours) earns .5 credits. I recommend you don't go higher or lower than this. Too many credits may make a student appear dishonest or unhealthy (he needs time to breathe and do something besides being a student). Fewer credits may lead admissions staff to think the student can't handle a normal academic load.

Some parents list core courses taken in the 8th grade for high school credit (Algebra 1, for example). That's fine, but it's not mandatory. If you list Algebra 2 on a transcript, colleges will know that your student completed Algebra I in the 8th grade. If you decide to grant credit for classes taken during 8th grade, make sure they're equivalent to high school-level courses, and don't lighten the load in subsequent years or, again, they may assume your student can't handle a normal course load.

If your student has several outside interests (theater, sports, etc.), and counting all of them as classes will push him over 32 credits, list them as extra-curricular activities on his college application. He will appear more well-rounded, without an overblown transcript.

You can schedule full courses over the length of the regular school year, or develop a block schedule and compress a full course into a semester (or block). Students on block schedules spend twice as much time each day on their classes each block, but still devote 150-180 hours total on each subject.

Many homeschoolers use a mixed schedule, compressing some classes into blocks, and letting others span the entire school year. If you schedule regular semester .5 credit classes, such as government and economics, don't double the time spent on them since they typically earn only half a credit.

If you decide to use a block schedule for some (or all) of your classes, assign subjects that build on each other (mathematics, foreign language, etc.) back to back. If you leave large breaks between them (for example, Spanish 1 in fall of 9th grade, Spanish 2 in the spring of 10th grade), your student will forget previously learned material and waste a lot of time reviewing.

If possible, develop a tentative four-year course plan before your student begins his freshman year so he can realistically achieve his college or career goals. If you begin homeschooling mid-high school, include previous classes your student has already taken, and build from there.

What courses are required for graduation?

Each state has its own graduation requirements. If yours doesn't require specific subjects for homeschoolers, you're free to design your own course plan. Work together with your student to develop courses that will help him achieve his goals after graduation.

If he's college-bound, research the schools he's interested in attending to see what they require for admission. Plan his courses around those requirements, but keep in mind that colleges often allow deviations, especially if a student excels in a unique subject, has an intriguing talent or interest, or scores particularly well on their college entrance exam (SAT or ACT).

If your student doesn't plan to go to college, cover core subjects like history, science, mathematics, and writing, but also include courses and apprenticeships that will help him get ahead in his chosen career field (woodworking, auto mechanics, sales, machining, photography, journalism, computer science, etc.). If he's planning to start his own business after graduation, include courses on how to manage a business (bookkeeping, financing, marketing, taxes, etc.).

For students who are undecided about the future, start with courses that meet typical graduation requirements (in case college turns out to be the goal), then adjust from there as interests become more defined. Most states require three or four courses each in the areas of English, mathematics, and natural sciences; and two courses each in social studies and foreign language. That still leaves a lot of room for electives, so try to balance academic subjects with those that may be more enjoyable for your student (art, theater, music, photography, computer science, forensics, sports, volunteerism, etc.). One of these electives or volunteer experiences may develop into a career opportunity.

Whatever your student decides to do after high school, I caution you (and your student) not to think of one path as "less than" another. Society often looks at college as "better," but it may not be better for your student. I know plenty of people with degrees who are either unemployed or have jobs that don't require the degree they worked so hard to get, and paid so much for. I also know plenty of college graduates who are happy and successful in their fields, so I'm not discouraging anyone from going to college. I just want to reassure you (and your student) that he can be happy and successful with his own choices and goals, whatever they may be.

I need help with course descriptions and titles.

If you use textbooks, and your state or homeschool organization requires you to describe your classes, copy the descriptions the publisher provides in their catalog. If you use other resources (literature studies, documentaries, field trips, internships, etc.), search the internet for high school course catalogs (many schools post them on their websites). Use their descriptions as templates, but tweak them to fit your own courses.

When deciding on course titles, make sure they're short enough to fit neatly on a one-page transcript. Instead of "Literature of the Ancient Period," for example, use "Ancient Literature." Traditional course titles work fine (English I, Algebra I) and are easily understood by college admissions staff, but don't shy away from non-traditional titles. You'd be amazed at the courses available now in high schools across the country—Forensic Science, Criminal Justice, Dance, Poetry, Television & Film, Drama, and Mystery Writing are just a few of the titles I found while researching.

Here are more suggestions to get you started:

English/Literature/Language Arts
English I, English II, English III, English IV—composition, grammar, vocabulary, and literature are studied each year and are usually covered under these titles (the emphasis on grammar lessens each year, in my experience). Other literature and writing electives not

typically covered in the English I-IV sequence (and require separate study) are: Classical Literature, Ancient Literature, Mythology, Mystery and Suspense, Holocaust Literature, Shakespeare, Expository Writing, Poetry, Writing the Novel, Business Writing, Short Stories, etc.

Science/Technology
Biology, Chemistry, Physical Science, Physics, Astronomy, Oceanography, Marine Science, Geology, Forensic Science, Computer Science, Keyboarding, Programming, etc.

Mathematics
Algebra I, II, Geometry, Trigonometry, Pre-Calculus, Calculus, Statistics, Consumer Math, Business Math, Advanced Math

Foreign Language
Latin, Spanish, French, German, American Sign Language, and other foreign languages. (Most colleges require at least two years in the same language. Some colleges don't accept Latin and American Sign Language as a foreign language.)

History/Social Studies
US History, World History, Western Civilization, European History, Ancient History
Psychology, Sociology, Criminal Justice
Government, Economics, Civics
Current Events, Contemporary Issues
Philosophy

Business/Vocational
Automotive, Machine Shop, Welding
Entrepreneurship, Small Business, Office Management
Electronics, Plumbing

Other/Electives
Physical Education
Driver's Education
Photography
Home Economics
Child Development
SAT/ACT Prep

Volunteer Service/Apprenticeships
With a local business: Career Education
With a veterinarian: Veterinary Studies
With horses: Equestrian Studies
On a farm: Agricultural Science
On a farm or ranch: Animal Husbandry
With a local newspaper: Journalism
With local radio or TV station: Broadcast Journalism
Etc…

How do I grant credits?

You can grant credits based on hours of study, textbook completion, or a course contract (or a combination of the three). If you use textbooks, reading the chapters and completing assignments equals one credit.

For courses where there are fewer assignments or tests to base a credit on (such as music, physical education, community volunteerism, or apprenticeships), counting hours may be the easiest option. Decide how many hours you want to require for course completion (usually 150 to 180), and grant credit when the student completes the required amount of time engaged in the activity.

For other non-textbook courses, the best method may be a contract between you and your student, clearly stating expectations you've both agreed on. Grant a credit when he completes the specific requirements listed in the contract.

Some courses are traditionally granted only half a credit (Economics and Government are two examples). They are completed in half the time (around 75 to 90 hours) or have less involved texts, so adjust your expectations to fit these shorter courses.

Don't discount practical experience when granting credits. Most teens will earn a credit in computer science without doing anything other than what they already do (word processing, keyboarding, working with database or excel files, internet research, gaming, graphics, building a website or maintaining a blog, networking, social media, etc.).

If they're actively involved in organized sports, they'll easily earn a credit for physical education without doing anything extra. Students who aren't as sports-minded can also easily earn a credit by completing an exercise program incorporating walking, running, Wii Fit, swimming, lifting weights, hiking, or similar activities.

Those are just a few examples of how you can turn everyday life into credit-earning experiences. Learning happens all the time, so make sure you don't overlook what your children are already accomplishing.

How do I determine grades?

Textbook-oriented courses designed for homeschoolers will often have grading guidelines in the teacher's guide. You can use these guidelines, or establish your own grading system.

If you use a course contract as described in the previous section, your student's grade will be determined by how many assignments he successfully completes. He'll earn an "A" if he completes all assignments on time and to the standards you both agreed on. One or two late or sub-standard assignments will earn a B; and so on. Include your grading guidelines in the contract so your student is aware upfront of what he must do to earn a good grade. If your student earns credit through volunteer service or an apprenticeship, ask his supervisor for help with grading his experience.

Experts in the field (or someone who teaches the subject) may be able to provide assistance if you need help evaluating your student's work. When my oldest son's interest in ancient history and classical literature went well beyond my own, I asked teachers on a homeschool-friendly Latin internet discussion list to help me with his grades.

I had intended to give him a semester's (.5) credit for mythology, and a full credit in ancient history. However, when I gave the teachers his reading list and details about his studies, they told me I was actually short-changing him. His work went way beyond the 1.5 credits I thought he'd earned, so they encouraged me to give him a full credit each for mythology, ancient history, and classical literature. Then they helped me grade each course.

If your student is studying a subject which has a specialized national (or international) exam, encourage him to take it. His score may give you additional insight on a suitable grade for the course. My oldest son took the National Latin Exam (www.nle.com) and the Medusa Mythology Exam (www.medusaexam.org), both of which are rigorous and highly regarded. Since I didn't give him tests for those courses, his achievement on the exams validated the high grades I gave him, and the awards he received looked great on his college scholarship applications.

If you're uncomfortable asking teachers for help, or can't find one who is friendly to homeschoolers, search the internet for high school websites. Teachers often post their class syllabi online, and you can use their course requirements and grading scales as a reference when evaluating your student's work.

Regardless of the method you use for grading, don't forget to involve your student in the evaluation process. Begin with his best subject and agree on the grade for that course. Then discuss the next subject, agreeing on the grade he earned relative to his best course, and work your way down to the course he spent the least amount of time and effort on.

In the end, grading will be subjective unless you use a standardized curriculum, with objective fill-in-the blank or multiple-choice assignments and tests. Don't sacrifice an interesting, educational, and challenging curriculum (even if you have to put it together yourself) just because it'll be more difficult to grade objectively. A grade is just number. Learning the material is what really matters.

When you assign grades, follow the grading scale your state uses. Colleges and employers in your area that request a transcript will be most familiar with the state's grading system, and may not accept anything different. The state's grading scale may also be required if your student is applying for state-sponsored scholarships.

A typical scale is: 93-100=A; 85-92=B; 77-84=C; 70-76=D; 0-69=F. Each number grade will then be awarded quality points based on the type of course: College or Tech Prep, Honors, or Advanced Placement (AP) and International Baccalaureate (IB). Most of your student's courses will be weighted as College Prep or Tech Prep. Honors courses are often weighted at half a point higher than College or Tech Prep, with AP and IB courses weighted a full point higher.

Some states also weight dual enrollment courses (college courses taken while a student is still in high school) higher than College/Tech Prep courses, but not as high as AP or IB courses.

Research your state's guidelines to see how they determine quality points for each course.

Honors courses should meet substantially higher requirements than a regular high school course. They should also be in a core subject area. Physical Education listed as an honors course will probably raise eyebrows. If your student is gifted in sports, show it in his list of extra-curricular activities and note any sports awards he's received. That will be more meaningful (and believable) to admissions staff.

AP and IB credit is not usually awarded unless your student has attended an actual AP or IB class and/or passed the exam for the course. Don't list courses as AP or IB unless you have proof they took the classes and/or passed the exams.

When you research your state's grading scale, it will most likely include information about computing a final grade point average (GPA). If not, consider purchasing transcript software that will calculate this for you, or find an experienced parent or teacher to help you. Don't submit a transcript until you verify your student's grades, quality points, and GPA are correct.

I'll end this section with a final bit of advice—don't list all 100's on your student's transcript. Everyone, including your student, has strengths and weaknesses and his grades need to reflect that. If they don't, his transcript will likely be viewed as less credible, especially if he has average (or lower) test scores on the SAT or ACT (college entrance exams). If his scores don't coincide with what's listed on the transcript, colleges may ask for more documentation to substantiate his grades. So make sure your student's grades reflect his ability and achievement, and that they're consistent with standardized test results.

Can my high school student take college courses?

Most colleges allow high school students to enroll in their classes. These courses are usually weighted the same as an honors course.

There are several benefits to dual enrollment: it leaves fewer classes for parents to plan for, students gain experience completing assignments on a schedule determined by someone outside of the family, and they become more comfortable with the college environment while their course load is relatively light.

Probably the biggest benefit, however, is the opportunity for your student to become acquainted with one or more professors. When he applies for scholarships that require a reference, his professor may provide one for him. Faculty recommendations often carry more weight and could result in a better scholarship.

How do we prepare for college entrance exams?

Bright students should consider taking the PSAT (www.collegeboard.org) in their junior year. If they score high enough, they'll have a chance of being awarded a National Merit Scholarship (www.nationalmerit.org/nmsp.php). Scholarship winners usually receive additional funds, resulting in four tuition-free years at the college of their choice.

Since only a small percentage of test-takers become National Merit finalists, most students focus instead on preparing for the SAT (www.collegeboard.org) or the ACT (www.act.org), beginning in their junior year. These exams are required by most colleges for admission and scholarships. A few months of study and familiarization with test strategies can substantially increase your student's scores.

The SAT has three main parts: critical reading (reading passages and sentence completions), math (algebra, geometry, statistics, and probability), and writing (25-minute essay, grammar, and usage).

To prepare for the critical reading section, your student should read often and in a variety of genres. Students who are readers will likely score well in this area without further study (other than familiarizing themselves with the types of questions on the test). In my experience, this is one area a student can't "cram" for.

For the writing and math sections, SAT prep books such as Barron's, Gruber's, and the College Board's SAT Study Guide are essential. I'd recommend purchasing at least two prep books to get better coverage (they vary in presentation and in difficulty of the practice problems).

Your student should read the section that explains the test format, then work through all of the instructional material. After he finishes, encourage him to take as many practice tests as he can stand, following strict timed test conditions. When he takes the real test, he'll know what to expect and will spend his time answering the questions instead of wasting it on reading directions.

The SAT is offered throughout the year at different schools and test centers. Students should take it for the first time no later than spring of their junior year. If they don't score well, they can retake it in the summer, or in the fall of their senior year. This should give them plenty of time to receive their scores before any admissions and scholarship deadlines.

The ACT tests the areas of English, math, reading, science, and has an optional writing section. I'm less familiar with it, but the general consensus is that it's less aptitude-based, and more focused on achievement. From what I've read, students often do better on one test or the other, so if your student doesn't do well on the SAT practice tests, try the ACT instead. Prepare the same way as I described above, using prep books and practicing under timed test conditions.

How do we pay for college?

I'm going to go out on a limb here and recommend against getting any student loans if you can possibly avoid it. I've met too many students (and parents who cosigned loans) with ruined credit because of unpaid student loans. The jobs weren't there after graduation, but the debt didn't wait. And, job or not, your student will spend many years paying off the loans.

Before accepting loans, your student should invest time preparing for the SAT or ACT so he'll score well enough to get state-funded or college-sponsored scholarships. Get a calendar and keep track of test dates, scholarship application deadlines, etc. Take advantage of any grants that are offered, such as PELL grants, state grants, or lottery funds if your state has an education lottery (and you aren't morally opposed to accepting those funds). Make sure your student double-checks before signing anything to make sure he's actually receiving grants and not loans.

Grants are usually awarded based on financial need, so there is no obligation to repay. Need is based on many factors, including parent income, student income, number of dependents, number of family members in college, and other factors. Don't automatically assume you won't qualify.

You'll most likely be required to fill out a FAFSA (Free Application for Federal Student Aid—www.fafsa.ed.gov). Complete this as soon as you're finished doing your taxes in January (you must do your tax return first). Their online form is easier than it used to be, and it can import much of the information it needs from your income tax return.

Many colleges award grants on a first-come, first-served basis, depending on your need score (Estimated Family

Contribution, or EFC) on the FAFSA. Once the funds run out, they're gone for that year, so remember to complete this as soon as possible in January after you finish your taxes.

If your student doesn't qualify for scholarships or need-based grants, a part-time job over the summer would likely pay for a couple of classes at the local community college. Many smaller, local colleges have transfer agreements with state universities, so credits will transfer into a degree program at a fraction of the cost. If he does well in his classes, he may then qualify for academic scholarships the next semester, or the following year.

If student loans are unavoidable, accept the smallest amount your student can get by with. They add up faster than you realize, and will hit your student all at once when he graduates.

Will my student get a high school diploma from the state?

Probably not. Most states don't award diplomas to students graduating from a homeschool (or a private school, for that matter). Only their public school graduates get state diplomas. Your student will still be a high school graduate, but he'll most likely receive his diploma from you, or from a homeschool organization that you've registered with. Visit www.homeschooldiploma.com or similar websites to order homeschool diplomas, graduations invitations, and more.

Part VI—Dealing with Problems

My friends and family are trying to talk me out of homeschooling. What should I do?

Don't discuss homeschooling with them anymore. Explain that you have an unfair advantage over them because you've researched the benefits of homeschooling, and they haven't. Offer to talk about your decision with them once they finish researching the subject as much as you have.

Provide them with a list of homeschooling books, magazines, websites, and articles so they can read about it for themselves. Then wait to see if they accept your offer. My guess is they won't. It's much easier to criticize your choice than to learn the facts for themselves.

Once you've made your stand, it's important not to let yourself get drawn into homeschooling discussions with them until they've read at least several of the references on your list. Be kind, but firm, saying something along the lines of, "I understand you just want the best for little Johnny because you love him. I love him, too, and that's why I decided to homeschool. Have you read any of the resources I suggested? No? Well, I look forward to talking to you about it, so let me know when you do!" Then smile and change the subject.

If they try to bring you back to the discussion, remind them you have an unfair advantage and will wait until they have a chance to research it, then change the subject again. You'll have to be consistent, and it may take a while, but they'll eventually give up or read the research and become converts themselves.

My husband isn't on board with homeschooling. How can I convince him this is right for us?

Try to ease him into it. Offer to give him books, articles, or websites to read so he can become more comfortable with the idea. If he's still against it after reading more about it, offer to give it a trial run for one year. Assure him you'll both evaluate how things are going at the end of the year before deciding whether or not to continue.

Usually that's all it takes. Your husband will be able to see the benefits of homeschooling for himself and be more supportive.

If the idea of a trial run isn't quite enough to sway him, offer to test the children at the end of the year. If their scores are average or above, that should reassure him they're performing at least as well as public school students. I suggest you use testing only as a last resort. It can cause stress for everyone, and it really has nothing to do with learning.

We're on a tight budget right now and can't afford to spend much money on curriculum. Can we still homeschool?

Yes. You don't need an expensive curriculum to homeschool. One of my favorite resources is my library card. I can get a world-class education by reading (or listening to) all the books, movies, and magazines available to me for free.

Museums, zoos, aquariums, and historical sites often have free or "budget" days, when admission is half-price or less. Educational documentaries are available from PBS, Discovery Channel, Animal Planet, etc. Many more free or low-cost resources are recommended in the Curriculum & Resources section of this book.

If you're looking for specific materials, many local and state support groups have used curriculum sales throughout the year. You can also ask local families if they have resources they no longer need.

If you can't find anything locally, many homeschoolers sell their used items on internet message boards. Although it can be risky to send money to people you don't know, most buyers don't have any problems and find the risk worth the savings. Try homeschoolclassifieds.com and welltrainedmind.com/forums.

My child has special needs. Can we still homeschool?

Absolutely. Many parents are able to work around their student's special needs more easily in a homeschool setting. Although well-intentioned professionals may encourage you to keep your child in school to access their services, you'll likely be able to find support from other homeschool parents who have experience with special needs. They'll know which public services are available to homeschoolers in your area, and also recommend private service providers, if needed.

My friends, family, and even strangers try to quiz my children to see how much they're learning. It makes us uncomfortable. What can I do?

I don't think people realize how much quizzing bothers children (whether they're homeschooled or not). Being asked to "prove" their knowledge would make even most adults squirm. While we can refuse to "perform," children feel trapped into it because we teach them to be polite.

When this happens again, politely explain that you don't allow people to quiz your children because it makes them feel as if they're on display. You can leave it at that and change the subject, or offer to make an exception if they'll allow the children to quiz them first. Most people won't accept the challenge, realizing just how uncomfortable it is to be put on the spot. In case they do, prepare questions beforehand that your children can ask (the more difficult and obscure, the better).

Help your children come up with their own strategies to handle situations when you're not around. Maybe something like, "Oh, are we playing a trivia game? Cool! Let us go first!" They can then ask the questions they've prepared and diffuse the situation by making a game out of it.

My mom constantly raves about the great things her other grandchildren are learning in public school. I try to tell her what my kids are doing, but she doesn't want to hear it. What should I do?

It sounds like your mom disapproves of homeschooling and is trying to undermine your confidence by making public school seem so much better. Her goal is to manipulate you into enrolling your children in school, but not be blamed for interfering. She'd rather claim it was all your idea.

Now that you know her intentions, it's very easy to stop her—just don't play along. When she brags about other children, act just as thrilled as she is. Say something like, "Really?! That's great!" and change the subject to something else.

Don't be surprised when she keeps trying to get a reaction out of you. Just be consistent with your responses: "Wow! That's interesting!" or "You don't say?!" or something else that means absolutely nothing. Then keep changing the subject.

She'll eventually stop trying to manipulate you, or she'll be honest and tell you she wants you to stop homeschooling. Then you can finally discuss her concerns openly.

A homeschool friend told me I'll shortchange my children if I don't use "ABC" curriculum, but I prefer something else.

Her attitude reflects her own subconscious insecurities—the more people she talks into using "ABC," the more it reinforces her belief it's the perfect curriculum. She's sincerely trying to help, but there's no such thing as one "perfect" curriculum. Each family is different, and each child is different. What works for one may not work for another.

I'm sure many homeschoolers have gone on to college or started successful careers after using "ABC" curriculum, but just as many have gone on to greater heights using something different, or no packaged curriculum at all.

Trust me on this one. Choose your resources based on your children's needs, not someone else's insecurities.

I can't find a local support group. How can I meet other homeschoolers?

When I began homeschooling over twenty years ago, it was still a relatively new concept for most people. Fewer families were doing it, and fewer resources were available. Most textbook companies wouldn't even sell to homeschoolers back then, and the general population usually assumed we were members of a cult, or religious fanatics, or religiously fanatic cult members. (Sorry, I couldn't resist. No disrespect intended to fanatics or cult members, religious or otherwise.)

The one thing that saved us was the pioneering spirit that bound us together. Local groups were numerous and active because we needed each other for support and information.

Over the past several years, many local groups have slowly dwindled or disappeared altogether. Even statewide groups are struggling, finding it difficult to provide the same services to their shrinking memberships. A state group in my region recently stopped mailing print newsletters and voted to drop their yearly homeschool conference after holding one for over 20 years. It's not because there are fewer homeschoolers; it's our support network that's changing.

One factor contributing to this change is the internet. Social media websites, discussion lists, message boards, and chat rooms have enabled homeschoolers to share information about new resources, learning methods, special needs, and more, without leaving the comfort of their pajamas.

State-funded virtual charter schools, tuition-based co-operatives, and "hybrid schools" (a mix of homeschooling and onsite classes) have also had a dampening effect on local groups. On the one hand, they've provided more alternatives for families who want to keep their children home, but feel the need for more outside help and accountability. On the other hand, they've contributed to a growing tendency among homeschoolers to spend so much time focused on academics, little time is left over for their children to play, talk, and just be together.

I've noticed this trend even on my group trips, where some of my families spend their free time each evening in their hotel rooms doing "school work," while the other children (and parents) are in the lobby, getting to know each other and talking about the sites they visited that day.

To see if others have noticed the same trends, I conducted a poll at my website asking families where they got most of their support. Out of the 405 people who responded, the majority (41%) said the internet (social media sites, message boards, etc.) provided most of their support, while another 18% cited academic co-operatives or organizations. Only 30% said they received support from a local support group that didn't have an educational focus. The remaining respondents indicated they didn't need support for their homeschooling (3%), or had other (mostly undefined) means of support (8%).

These results mirror what I've seen. The internet and organized academic programs now have the biggest role in supporting homeschoolers, while purely social groups are a minority. Here are some of the comments from parents who answered my poll:

I would love to have homeschool groups and co-ops for additional support, but there just doesn't seem to be a big homeschool community in my area. It's to the point where we're considering relocation to another area. —Elizabeth, South Carolina

We have a large homeschooling population in our area, but there is not much support for secular homeschoolers. Most of my support comes from a small group of individuals that I have gotten to know personally and the internet support groups and boards that I am a member of. —Beth, South Carolina

When I started out with a preschooler and kindergartner, the support group newsletter was a huge help (field trips, class opportunities, discounts, etc.) but now I use Facebook, message boards, and Yahoo groups. —Shelley, Texas

It seems it's harder to find physical groups for support anymore in my area. Everyone goes the internet route or they have joined charter schools. I've found that for my high-school-age kids, there are no support groups. I pretty much go it alone now. Also, the fact that I work full-time makes it harder. I definitely rely on internet groups at this point for myself. It's kind of sad not to have physical groups.—Debi, Utah

I feel so blessed to have found a fantastic group in my area. My husband wants to move back to Tampa, but the major reason I don't want to is because of my homeschool support group. I would rather each of us keep driving an hour to work! —Tammy, Florida

I have a wonderful group of friends who have paved the road for me. I could not do it without them. —Stacy, North Carolina

There seem to be a plethora of homeschool groups here in Indiana. My advice is to find a few friends who have similar values and educational philosophy. I find that the larger groups don't allow for the close relationships my kids are looking for. It is quite a balancing act for our family to do all of their activities and socializing. When I mentor or speak to newbies, the question I'm asked most often is "are your kids socialized?" Uh, yes, to the point that we have trouble keeping the "home" in homeschooling. —Lisa, Indiana

So, to answer the original question, support is out there, it'll just take a little more work to find it if you're not part of an established academic program or group. Look for notices in your local newspaper, or ask your state homeschool organization for a list of groups. If you can't find one in your city, consider starting one by posting notices in your local paper and on your state organization's website or newsletter. There *are* families looking for local support (I get emails from them every day), so it may not be as difficult to start a group as you may think.

Part VII—Favorite Articles

My House is a Mess!
by Kim Blum-Hyclak

My house is a mess. I want to get down to the business of
schoolwork with my children, but the clutter is getting in the
way. Colorful Legos dot the floor like land mines ready to be
stepped on. Books have escaped the prison of the shelves and lay
open, hiding in freedom in the stairway alcove. The box of craft
supplies exploded and the debris lies in creative concentric
circles. The two dishes I left in the sink last night mated. Their
offspring now enjoy the run of the table and the counter top.
The piles of laundry I lovingly folded now lean like a famous
monument, inching their way to the edges of the washer and
dryer.

I survey the damage and feel overwhelmed. I yearn for the
day when I can sit at the table with my kids and their lessons and
open their minds to all the wonderful "stuff" the world has to
offer, without the distractions that our daily living heaps upon us.

But after years of homeschooling, I know this is not the
dream I want realized. I am living my dream. The Legos are not
just creations, they are lighthouses. They are modeled after the
lighthouse we visited on a trip to Florida. In one afternoon at
Ponce Inlet, we learned about the inlet and its lighthouse,
climbing its 203 steps to the top. We toured buildings packed
with exhibits and learned about how the lighthouse works and its
history, about lighthouses around the world, about ocean life and

what it's like to be a sailor, about how Cuban refugees escape to America and the courage it must take.

The books in the alcove had help escaping. There is never a complete set of encyclopedias on the shelves; my children squander them in their rooms. The delinquent books in the alcove are the remainders of the journey my children took looking for Alaska. There is "w" for world, "u" for universe, "m" for maps, and finally "a" for Alaska. Along their journey, I know they also found many surprises.

The other books scattered about are the pleasure books that I have to pry from their hands when it is time for bed. There are the lighthouse books and my ninth-grader's John Grisham from the library. There is the young teen book my daughter absorbs, opening the door to questions and discussions that take place at the dinner table or wherever she needs.

Out of the creative explosion of the craft box comes a colorful "ojos de Dios," eyes of God. My son has given me this offering to place alongside the other gifts of my children's handiwork. Like an archeological dig, my bookcase and shelves are lined with artifacts from our various studies. There is the Egyptian pitcher molded from clay, the heraldry shield with our family crest, the quilt sampler from our American Girls Quilting Circle. There is pride in their workmanship and love in their offering.

The dishes were a lesson in science. Mixing water and flour makes paste. Mixing bouillon and water makes a solution. Heat from the stove causes a chemical reaction, the liquid of eggs becoming solid. They are also a lesson in math—figuring the correct amounts for a recipe and the correct time for cooking. Full meals have been cooked in my absence, including pasta sauce from scratch. The three kids help each other and divide the tasks.

The clothes would have been put away if we hadn't had a field trip to the state park for a program on birds. They would have gotten put away later, but we had to meet with other homeschoolers for a Lenten activity. Later that night, they were still patiently waiting to be tended to, but I was playing Monopoly and reading to my children.

I would like my house to be neat and tidy, but now is not the time. Webster defines education as "the development of knowledge, skill, ability, or character by training, study, or experience." He defines "learning" as "the gaining of knowledge or skill." In our homeschool, we do this in the distractions of our lives, not exclusive of them.

My children have taken responsibility for a portion of their education and taken it out of the boundaries of the kitchen table. As I write this, my older son does Latin and Algebra in his bedroom. My daughter is reading on the deck. My third is in the clubhouse with the dog, writing a story with the words he knows how to spell. Work is still done at the kitchen table, but most of the learning is done around the house. And it is done in an environment that not only encourages, but expects them to be respectful, compassionate, helpful, and encouraging to each other.

These lessons, now being applied to someone older or younger, or of another sex, will easily transfer to others of a different race, culture, or religion. This is what education is all about—taking what is being learned and assimilating it into their everyday playing and living. So yes, my house is a mess, but more importantly, at this point, my children are not.

About the author

Kim Blum-Hyclak homeschooled three of her five children for over 20 years. She saw many changes in her homeschooling years, from needing to seek permission to homeschool from the local school board and being advised to keep her children inside during the school day, to being on the board of one of the original Option 3 homeschool associations in South Carolina. She still believes homeschooling was one of the most rewarding experiences she and her children had.

Her youngest will begin his final year at the University of South Carolina in the fall of 2012, where he currently works. Her middle child has worked as a nanny for the past several years. Her oldest graduated from USC School of Law in May of 2012 and will begin clerking for the York County, SC Circuit Court Judge in August. When her homeschooling years came to an end, Kim revived her writing aspirations and still enjoys learning—even without the kids going along.

Gabrielle's Journey

by Kim Blum-Hyclak

My daughter, Gabrielle, graduated several years ago. She had been homeschooled from the beginning, not conforming to the boundaries of a typical education.

As a family, we started our homeschooling adventure under the philosophy of John Holt, a pioneer in the homeschool movement. We agreed that children have a natural curiosity. Given the right tools, environment, and encouragement, children can learn what they need to know without much "help" from us. We allowed Gabrielle, as well as her siblings, to follow their interests and have not been disappointed in their academic endeavors. Sometimes frustrated, but never disappointed!

While not following a typical "college preparatory" curriculum, Gabrielle still managed to earn all the necessary credits for graduation, and more. She had always known that college was an option, but not the only one. Her interests and her heart had always been in ministry, and that's the path her high school studies prepared her for.

After high school, Gabrielle followed her heart and began working in youth ministry. She was accepted for the National Evangelization Team (NET), sponsored by the Catholic Church. She spent five weeks in Minnesota, learning various skits, honing her small group techniques, and becoming a part of her traveling retreat team.

Her team, consisting of ten young adults ages 18-25 and a couple of adult chaperones, spent the following nine months living out of suitcases and backpacks. Luckily, Gabrielle was rather petite, so her clothes didn't take up a lot of room. She had a storage cabinet at NET headquarters to store her seasonal clothing since she wouldn't know from one month to the next where she would be.

Gabrielle's team traveled throughout the United States, putting on retreats for junior and senior high youth. The length of the retreats varied from one night to all weekend, but most nights involved a different city, a different parish, and a different group of teens than the night before. Host families at each stop fed and lodged the team. She soon learned that she better like Sloppy Joes and pizza!

Gabrielle eagerly looked forward to that next phase of her journey, both the literal one and the figurative one. She knew the world extended beyond the county line and couldn't wait to see new parts of the country. She had grown up in South Carolina and had experienced Ohio winters, but not Minnesota winters! She hoped to get the chance to visit New York and California, and was looking forward to seeing the varied cultures our diverse country holds.

What would happen after NET? She wasn't sure. All she was sure of is that God would let her know.

What happened after NET?

Gabrielle has worked as a nanny for the past several years and currently takes care of two children. She's also still involved with her church teaching Confirmation classes.

About the author

Kim Blum-Hyclak homeschooled three of her five children for over 20 years. She saw many changes in her homeschooling years, from needing to seek permission to homeschool from the local school board and being advised to keep her children inside during the school day, to being on the board of one of the original Option 3 homeschool associations in South Carolina. She still believes homeschooling was one of the most rewarding experiences she and her children had.

Her youngest will begin his final year at the University of South Carolina in the fall of 2012, where he currently works. Her middle child (the subject of this article) has worked as a nanny for the past several years. Her oldest graduated from USC School of Law in May of 2012 and will begin clerking for the York County, SC Circuit Court Judge in August. When her homeschooling years came to an end, Kim revived her writing aspirations and still enjoys learning—even without the kids going along.

Raise Children with a Wild Streak

by Mark Pruett

A new report from the American Academy of Pediatrics stresses the importance of childhood playtime. It reinforces my own belief that many young adults have been cheated by years of excessive schoolwork and teamwork, too many extracurricular activities, and a straitjacketed "just say no to anything risky" upbringing. I am convinced that modern childhood generally does not build enough independence and thirst for knowledge.

For the past few years I helped interview high school seniors seeking scholarships to come to Appalachian State University. These applicants come from all over the state. They play instruments and sports, participate in church and charity, and work in diverse jobs.

They also display remarkably similar accomplishments. They are at the top of their high school classes and possess generically good manners. They lead teams, groups and clubs. They are smart, solid and hardworking.

They might be surprised to learn that I, like many college professors, yearn for rarer traits—curiosity, passion, a wild streak. Yes, teamwork and leadership skills will help your child to implement someone else's ideas, and extensive extracurricular activities will foster responsibility. What your child really needs, though, is an inventive, self-reliant, restless spirit.

The key questions

For me, the heart-wrenching interview moment is when we ask these teenagers what they would choose to do on a day spent alone. Many say they never have the chance. Worse still, some have no answer at all. This should disturb and sadden any parent. In the end, my scholarship votes ride on two questions: Is this someone that I'd be excited to have in my class? And is he or she open to being changed by my class? Class rank and extracurricular activities are less important than genuine individuality or enthusiasm. It matters not whether someone is bold or shy, worldly or naïve. Is there a flash of determination, a streak of independence, a creative passion, an excited curiosity?

We need more students like the ones who leave after graduation to work as missionaries or in the Peace Corps. More like the ones who start successful businesses while in school. More like the ones who find the courage to go overseas for a summer or a semester because they know their own worlds are far too small.

Some students are team players and high achievers, but I'd trade them for stubbornly creative iconoclasts. Some students as children were taught to color inside the lines, watch Barney the purple dinosaur, and always ask permission. We need students who found out what crayons tasted like, loved reading "The Cat in the Hat" and paid little attention to rules—students whose parents encouraged their children's curiosity.

Something's missing

The irony is that many students begin to perceive late in college that they've missed something along the way. They regret not taking risks with difficult professors, unusual courses or semesters abroad. They berate themselves by equating self-worth with grades, and they are saddened by the realization that they have only glimpsed the breadth of the university. They begin to grasp that their uncomfortable sense of passivity has its roots in the highly controlled existence foisted on them.

Parents: love, guide and support your children, but don't insulate them, control them or let them be too busy. Independence, confidence and creativity come from freedom, risk and a good measure of unstructured solitude.

Encourage studying but make them play hooky, too—partly to learn what it feels like to be unprepared and partly to foster spontaneity, irreverence and joy. Study chemistry together, then blow up a television in the backyard.

Foster camaraderie and connectedness through group activities (especially family ones), but be unyielding in your commitment to teaching them to love doing things entirely on their own. Make each child plan and cook the family's dinner on his or her own once a week.

Surround them with books, not video games. Raise a garden or build a deck together. Send them on solo trips.

However you choose to do it, give your children, their teachers and society one of the greatest gifts of all: help your kids become creative, independent, curious, interesting people.

About the author

Mark Pruett is an assistant professor of business and economics at the University of South Carolina—Upstate. Write to him at mpruett@uscupstate.edu. Reprinted with permission of the author and The Charlotte Observer. Copyright owned by The Charlotte Observer.

Afterword

Dear Reader,

I hope you enjoyed this book and found it helpful. If you have questions, comments, or suggestions for future updates, please email me at director@carolinahomeschooler.com. I look forward to hearing from you.

About the Author

Dianna Broughton is the director of Carolina Homeschooler, a support organization known for its group trips to Washington DC, New York City, Disney World, Italy, Alaska, and beyond. She has homeschooled her four children for over 20 years, with two still learning at home.

Contact Information

Carolina Homeschooler
PO Box 1421
Lancaster, SC 29721

Website Links

Website: www.carolinahomeschooler.com
Mailing List: carolinahomeschooler.com/acommunity.html
Facebook: facebook.com/carolinahomeschooler
Twitter: twitter.com/CarolinaHomesch
Pinterest: pinterest.com/carolinahomesch
Yahoo: groups.yahoo.com/group/CarolinaHomeschooler

CPSIA information can be obtained at www.ICGtesting.com
Printed in the USA
LVOW05s1445311013

359480LV00001B/155/P